THE WAITING
ROOM

TABLE OF CONTENTS

INTRO

Since this is our first time together, let me tell you a little about myself. My name is Kelly. I am the wife of my awesome husband, Calvin. Amai is my 16-year-old daughter, and Aubrey is my 7-year-old bonus daughter. When I started this writing process, I was a single mom in my 30s, and since I took so long, I've now been married for three years to a pretty awesome guy. While I grew up a bit privileged compared to most of the world, not everything came so easily for me. There have been so many times when my life felt like that movie "Failure to Launch." Try as I might, I felt as though I could not take off no matter how I tried. As much as I hate it, achieving any level of success in anything always seems to take so much longer for me than for many people I've encountered. I didn't even land my first real job until I was 28. When God spoke to me and told me to write about patience and waiting, I really thought He was kidding.

I began writing this with the feeling that I had absolutely no authority, but as I moved on in obedience (more like dragged my feet), I realized that all this waiting I'm always doing had to have a purpose bigger than just my little world, otherwise what would really be the point? But if all that I've learned and gone through in my seasons of waiting, matched with God's word, can make it a little easier for someone else, then it's all worth it.

This is not another book about waiting for marriage. When I started this journey, I was waiting to get out on my own. I was waiting to see the purpose God placed in me realized. And yes, I was waiting for marriage. I was in what seemed like a waiting room that I had no idea how to get out of. At some point, I got used to being in this waiting space, just sitting around and waiting for my life to begin.

I had no idea that this waiting room was actually more like a workshop. Life before this point had emptied me out. I had been broken down and worn out by life's disappointments. I'll say something you'll hear from any person following Jesus: He saw my broken pieces and emptiness as something He could work with, build up, and fill up with new and better things. So, in this waiting workshop, God began working on me and showed me that waiting is an active process, certainly not the passive one I presumed it to be. I hope you'll stick with me as I share everything God has poured into me during my time of waiting.

I once lived like a damsel in distress, locked up in a tower, waiting for someone to save me. My Prince Charming, so to speak. In my mind, life would start when he arrived. I could move out when I got married. I could walk into my purpose when I got married. I could begin to follow my dreams when I got married.

I could develop a deeper relationship with God when I got married. Marriage was in my future, but I was not living the life I was given at that moment. I was wasting my time. I wasn't seizing any opportunities to grow. In a way, I was using "waiting for Mr. Right" as an excuse to be paralyzed. I was stuck in a tower I was never meant to be in. But I put myself in that tower, and there was never a lock. I simply needed to walk out. I thank God for giving me a lightbulb moment. God reminded me that He is with me, standing strong as ever, and that there is so much that I am capable of with Him. He reminded me that I have been purposed for so much more. Right now.

You may not be waiting for Prince Charming or Mrs. Right, but are you currently locked in a tower, just waiting for someone to slay the dragon and save you? If God told you that you are supposed to be an entrepreneur, are you going to wait around for your 40-year-old boss to retire in hopes that one day, maybe you'll get his position? You may be waiting quite a while. Who put you in the tower, and who locked you in? It's more than likely you believed in a few lies that were fed to you based on social norms or whatever, and you walked into the tower, closed yourself into a comfortable cell, and locked yourself in. Somewhere along the lines, you believed that you could not do things because you didn't have what it took. Maybe no one like you has ever endeavored to do what you've been dreaming, and you may doubt your own ability to be the first. Maybe logistics just don't add up. Now you're stuck and don't know how to get out. But thank God for Jesus. He is our knight in shining armor.

He is ready for you to call on Him so He can give you the keys to your freedom.

"In my distress I prayed to the Lord, and the Lord set me free." Psalms 118:5

Having the keys doesn't mean you'll never have to wait again. Sorry to tell you this, but as long as we are living, we'll always be waiting and looking forward to something. What I am saying is that you can live in freedom now. Freedom to wait actively. You have the freedom to run after your goals. You have the freedom to live, enjoy life, and walk in your purpose even before that big thing happens in your life.

God has unlocked the doors, but it is up to you to walk out of the tower. We have the choice to pick up our God-given weapons and slay our own dragons. Yes, you can slay your own dragons. You don't have to be paralyzed in fear as you wait, and you don't have to be buried in doubt; you can wait patiently and actively. Action is the key. There are so many things we can and should be doing as we wait.

CHAPTER 1

WAITING, THE ACTION PLAN

"Be patient." "Don't worry; it'll happen for you. Just be patient." I swear, if I had a dollar for every time I heard these things, I would be so rich. I don't ever want to wait, but I know I must. It's just one of those facts about life. I find myself calling my kids impatient, especially when they are bugging me about something I am already working on. "Why are you asking for food while I'm making dinner? I am literally preparing exactly what you are asking for. I can't give you raw chicken and uncooked pasta. You have to wait. YOU HAVE TO BE PATIENT!" That sounds wildly familiar. I often wonder what God thinks every time we don't receive instant gratification for the things we ask for.

We're all waiting for something. Waiting for a job. Waiting for a spouse. Waiting for a family. Waiting for a home. Waiting for a raise. Just waiting for life to change. Too often, we focus on the wait rather than how we handle it. We're constantly calling out in anguish, "Come on, God!" and "When will I get there?" or "How long must I wait?" Sometimes it's "God, are you even listening?" We take a cue from this verse, Habakkuk 1:2: *"How long, O Lord, must I call for help? But you do not listen!"*

We all get the instruction to be patient, but what does that even mean, really? What are you doing in times of waiting? There has got to be some kind of guideline to make this all a bit easier, right? I really can't say if waiting and being patient are ever easy things to accomplish, but I can guarantee that the time spent during that wait could indeed be used more efficiently. Your wait could certainly be a fruitful time in your life. The question we should all ask, especially in the long waiting seasons, is, "What am I doing with my wait?" Since we are called to live in love (1 John 4:16), and love is patient (1 Corinthians 13:4), shouldn't we actively pursue patience as we wait? I think we should start by defining what patience is.

Patience: The capacity to accept or tolerate delay, trouble, or suffering without getting angry or upset.

Or

Quiet, steady perseverance; even-tempered care; diligence

No matter how many definitions you look at, none describes patience as sitting around and doing nothing until something happens. Man, oh man, was I guilty of that. I maintained my daily life, making absolutely no changes whatsoever, and assumed that if God had promised me things, I could sit and wait for those things to fall out of the sky with zero work from me. Then I would get mad at God when nothing was happening. Patience is not being upset that you have to wait; it is the ability to push through and maintain hope regardless of how long it takes or how hard it gets. And there is most certainly always a lot to be learned, gained, and sometimes lost in the waiting.

So again, what are you doing with your wait?

God gave some pretty great waiting instructions to His people in Jeremiah.

"This is what the Lord of the Heavens armies, the God of Israel, says to all the captives He has exiled from Jerusalem: "Build homes and plan to stay. Plant gardens, and eat the food they produce. Marry and have children. Then find spouses for them so you have many grandchildren. Multiply! Do not dwindle away! And work for the peace and prosperity of the city where I sent you into exile. Pray to the Lord for it, for its welfare will determine your welfare... Do not let your prophets and fortune tellers who are with you in the land of Babylon trick you. Do not listen to their dreams, because they are telling you lies in my name. I have not sent them," says the Lord, "You will be in Babylon for seventy years. But then I will come and do for you all the good things I have promised. And I will bring you home again. For I know the plans I have for you," says the Lord, "They are plans for good and not for disaster, to give you a future and a hope. In those days when you pray, I will listen. If you look for me wholeheartedly, you will find me. I will be found by you," says the Lord. "I will end your captivity and restore your fortunes. I

will gather you out of the nations where I have sent you and will bring you home again to your own land." Jeremiah 29:4-14

I only ever hear Jeremiah 29:11 quoted as a nice, feel-good verse, and we can throw out the rest, right? No. God told these people that they would be held captive for seventy years. Seventy Years! He told them to set up shop and live. He told them to grow and prosper right where they were. They did not have to wait to be released before they could begin to live free. Forgive me for comparing your wait to captivity, although I know that's how it feels at times. I pray that you will not be waiting for seventy years. This scripture has shown me that patience requires action. That explains why they say, "Have patience" or "Be patient." It is truly an action.

God gave His people clear instructions about what they should be doing during their season of waiting. I am confident that He has given each of us instructions for what we should be doing during our waiting times as well. But it is up to us to hear what God is instructing us to do and to decide what kind of attitude we will present as we wait and whether or not we will walk through this wait feeling defeated or filled with hope and victory. My goal, hope, and prayer are that the words presented to you here will help to change your posture and perspective as you wait for God's promises and the desires of your heart to be fulfilled. Maybe you'll be able to skip a few unnecessary hurdles on the road ahead of you.

One of the first things I learned on this journey of practicing the art of patience was to never pray for patience. No one told me this. I should've said, "Hey, God, grant me the ability to wait and be kind and expectant, but not for an extended period of time. Oh, and I'd like to not have to earn the ability through extensive trials. Amen." We've got to be specific, right? Ha. I'm unsure whether God would've laughed at that prayer. But I did it. I prayed for patience—one big blanket prayer, not about any specific circumstance. I thought I was praying a "good Christian" prayer. I know that this is where all the lovely waiting began. Trial by fire, so to speak. If you, too, have prayed for patience in error, you will likely be able to relate to much of what I have to say in the coming pages.

Waiting looks different for everyone. We all have different stories and walks, and our waiting periods will reflect that. For some, waiting can make you feel stuck, as though everything seems to stay the same no matter what you do, like complete stagnancy. For others, it feels like you're constantly getting beat down. Your wait may feel like you're sinking in quicksand. The harder you fight, the quicker you sink. I think I've experienced all of these feelings at some point or another. But each difficulty was set up for a lesson or for strengthening my character.

First things first, if God says it, He will do it. He more than likely will not give you a timeline or an ETA, but what He promised will happen in His perfect will and timing. He will make it happen. He will not back down or change His mind. Keep on walking with Him and accepting His instructions, and know that what is for you will be yours.

Doubt and, of course, the enemy will try to slide in and cause us to question. "Did God really say that?" "Has God forgotten me?" "Did He mean that for me, or was that for someone else?" "Does God even care?" Doubt is inevitable, but we can't allow it to move in, decorate, and get comfortable. Doubt will come, but you don't have to invite it in. Instead, choose to trust. We have to trust God and take His word as fact. Remember how much weight His words have. Seriously. When was the last time anybody opened their mouth and BANG! Universe. That is the God we are putting our faith and hope in. We can stand firm in confidence and with great hope and expectation that, no matter how long the wait, and come what may, God will come through.

There's another reason why patience requires action. It's like telling your kids to go do something productive while they wait for dinner to be made. Time always goes by much faster when we don't just sit and stare at the clock. Imagine how long a day at work would feel if you were watching the clock for 8 hours straight. That would be like cruel and unusual punishment. I know we've all been in a waiting room and sat staring at the door, even if just for a minute or so. Every time that door would open, you'd perk up, hoping that your name would be the one called next. You know very well that you see about five people in the room who were definitely there when you arrived. Even then, you get a little disappointed when you hear someone call for "Robert," because that is not your name. Then you go back to staring at the door, and your wait seems like an eternity.

There's a reason why there are always magazines in waiting rooms. Staying occupied always makes the wait seem at least somewhat shorter. The more engaged you are, the more time flies. I believe there is an overlooked reason why the Bible tells us to do good works. It's certainly not to earn God's favor or love, because He gives those freely. I do think that part of the reason is to keep us occupied in a healthy manner as we wait on the fulfillment of God's various plans for our lives. In doing so, we fill the time gaps between destinations by doing something productive while our character is being developed.

"So let's not get tired of doing what is good. At just the right time we will reap a harvest of blessings if we don't give up." Galatians 6:9

Constantly focusing on your desires while you wait for them to become reality can drive you nuts. It's like self-inflicted torture. You end up zooming in on what you don't have and how long it's taking and being completely puzzled about how to make it all happen, like now. I'm very guilty of this, way more than I should be. At one point, I would go on thinking about having a husband all day; at some point, I would likely start thinking about how I DID NOT have a husband. And then comes that downward spiral. Where is he? When is he coming? Am I doing something wrong? Then I would have to work to be pulled out of that long line of questioning and doubt. What is the point of that? And how much time did I waste falling down that pit as though I didn't have better ways to spend my time?

Instead of focusing on the lack, focus on the abundance. Focus on the things you can change instead of the things you can't. Rather than focusing on the husband I didn't have at the time, I could spend that time working on developing the relationships I did have. I could try to be the best mother possible. I could invest more in my family and friends. I know that the investments I make in what I do at the moment will make for a greater return on the things to come in the future.

Shifting the focus from the clock to what's already in front of you will help you stay encouraged while you wait. Try setting some short-term goals to achieve in the meantime, so you don't end up with an idle mind. If you're seeking a new position or career, why not put your best into your current position and maybe even develop some skills you could use in the desired job? If you're jobless (on purpose or otherwise), why not put that determination into taking care of the home you live in, even if you live with others? Even if no one quite appreciates what you're doing, God sees, and He knows all you are doing is getting you ready for what's next.

You may save yourself from so many mental battles by keeping yourself occupied during this time. You will be forced to keep your head up, as it's kind of impossible to get much done with your head hanging low.

"This is what the Lord of Heavens armies, the God of Israel, says to all the captives He has exiled to Babylon from Jerusalem,

"Build homes and plan to stay. Plant gardens and eat the food they produce... and work for the peace and prosperity of the city where I sent you into exile. Pray to the Lord for it, for its welfare will determine your welfare." Jeremiah 29:4-5;7

God put the Israelites to work. He knew how long their wait would be. He knew what the full benefits and results of the long wait would be. God knew they would be consumed by grief and discouragement if they sat and did nothing in those 70 years. He told them to grow during the wait. Set up shop and prosper right where they were. Start families and businesses. What God did not tell them to do was sit around wallowing in sadness because they had to wait so long to be free. What is God calling you to build or increase during your wait? He is absolutely giving you the time and space to grow. Focus on these things and prosper.

If you do find yourself with your head hanging low, look up. It's so easy to get caught up in and consumed by what we're waiting for. Tunnel vision ends up taking over. The eyes and mind get drawn to the end result. This is nice in theory, but that is until you fall on your face because you forget two important things.

One: Look where you're walking.

If you're a parent like myself, you may have gone through or are currently struggling with the period of time when your kid runs into things regularly. Or you often have to shield them from being run over. They get so focused on one thing that they stop looking in the direction they are walking, then BAM! They run into poles, trip on curbs, or bump into people. If your kid is like my lovely daughter Amai (around age 5), they run into every side view mirror in every parking lot. They get so excited by the sight of the playground that they miss the pole in their pathway.

Just because you can see what you want doesn't mean you can stop paying attention to the pathway. You'll miss some pretty great things if you're not aware of your steps. You may have some people to meet and even take with you on your way. You may be asked to help with a project that seems to have nothing to do with anything, but it could be good for you to have a sense of accomplishment about something while you're waiting, just to give you a little boost. On the other hand, keeping your head on a swivel and being aware of what's coming at you can save you. You'll be able to dodge all the distractions, dangers, and attacks that will try to keep you from where you're going.

Imagine the mall parking lot on Christmas Eve. By some miracle, you find a parking space somewhere way in the back. From there, you have a clear view of the entrance. Now picture walking through that parking lot while staring at those doors and never losing that gaze. Wait. You just got run over. You missed that crazy last-minute shopper speeding into the parking space you just started crossing.

Just because you can see the door you want to walk into doesn't mean you can stop paying attention to the pathway you're currently walking on. This is why God gave us peripheral vision and a neck that pivots. Not only can we look ahead to where we're going, but we can also be aware of our surroundings so we'll know when to take a turn, step over something, duck, or let someone pass.

So, what does this look like in regard to our desires? You might be dreaming of starting a company. If you're alert, you'll see when help is coming your way. You'll see the people in your life that may make this dream a reality. That shiesty person attempting to get chummy with you and steal your ideas won't make it very far. Don't overlook the blessings, mistakes, and learning lessons that are happening today, as they will help you maneuver towards and through what you desire. The road is certainly just as important as the destination.

Two: You are not walking alone.

This one is more important than the previous one. You are not in this by yourself. You're not even leading the way. You are actually a child in that crazy parking lot. Your Father is walking with you and has offered His hand for you to hold. He stands high above you and can see great distances ahead. He can see all the twists and turns you will have to take. He can see the puddle you're about to step in; He will help you get around it. He can see any present or potential danger that may come your way.

"Your word is a lamp to guide my feet and a light for my path." Psalms 119:105

If we must have tunnel vision, aim it at Jesus. Go where He leads, and trust Him. Letting go of Him would be dangerous, and you won't make it without Him. He holds on with a firm grip, even when we try to lead the way or go in the wrong direction. He holds us up as we approach the puddle that we aren't paying attention to. He knows how deep and dirty that puddle really is. God holds on and even corrects us if we don't see the obstacles or when we try to throw a tantrum. We may even try to run away, but still, He holds on. He is our perfect Father, and if we allow Him, He will get us right where we need to be every time.

Again, waiting is an action. In the next couple of chapters, my goal isn't exactly to make your waiting times a cakewalk. My hope is to help you grow in these seasons just as God continuously grows me in my wait times. I want to help you put some things that God has already given you to work to help you navigate the season you are in, or maybe walking into. Let's be honest; as soon as you get through one wait, another will immediately come.

CHAPTER 2

GOD'S TIMING... NOT YOURS

As I said before, there was a time when I thought my blessings had nothing to do with my efforts. I could just sit around and wait for my desires to fall into my lap. I also had times when I believed in my own mind that I was fully ready for what I was asking for and just needed God to get with the program and bring it on. It's absolutely bananas that we feel we can tell God when WE think WE'RE ready. We are masters in our own minds at instructing God on how things are and how our waiting should end in a way that works best for us. Really? I may have just heard God laugh.

God's timing is always the best. He sees all and knows all, and that includes knowing about every alternative outcome. Everything great and worth having requires great preparation. Have you ever seen a pregnant woman, or have you ever been pregnant yourself? The baby doesn't arrive fully formed the day after conception. Thank

God. God purposefully chose to take His time developing that baby. We don't pop out as fertilized eggs. The time given for a fetus to develop is meant for preparation for everyone involved. The baby is given time to form and grow so that he or she may survive when presented to the world. The mother is literally stretched to make room for the baby's growth. Thank God that doesn't happen instantaneously. She can't expect her baby to arrive in just a month simply because she wants to see her baby's face. She'd lose the very thing she wanted the most by trying to rush the process. The time spent waiting gives the family time to prepare. Time to buy clothes, diapers, baby furniture, etc. They can begin to prepare financially and mentally. But most of all, the love in their hearts can grow with hope and anticipation. Nine months is just the beginning. Stepping into God's promises often requires us to do the same things involved in giving birth, like growing, stretching, being uncomfortable, losing sleep, waiting, and labor.

Let's look at David, a man who did so many great things in his lifetime. A man after God's heart. Do you realize how long and how much David had to endure, from when Samuel anointed him as the next king to when he actually became king? He was overlooked by his own father and ridiculed by at least one, if not all, of his brothers. He slayed a giant. He was nearly killed by his boss on multiple occasions (and you thought your boss was bad). David lived on the run, battled armies, lost his best friend, and so much more, and THEN he became king. (1 Samuel 16–2 Samuel 2). That was a pretty rough wait, but it took all that time and all of those trials to build David's character and grow the attributes necessary for a king.

The Bible gives example after example of waiting stories. Abraham and Sarah had a pretty bleak situation. They had to wait 100 years for their only kid to come. Think of how long it took for the Israelites to be freed from the Egyptians (the delay in the desert was their own fault). The time and trials between the first prophecy of Jesus and His arrival. Jesus, Himself, had to wait about 30 years to be released to begin His ministry. If Jesus, God in the flesh, had to wait patiently, should we not be honored to follow His lead in patient endurance?

"Patient endurance is what you need now, so that you will continue to do God's will. Then you will receive all that He has promised." Hebrews 10:36

We have to figure out how to trust God's timing. Jumping ahead of God's plan is dangerous. It's like eating a piece of chicken that's only been in the oven for ten minutes when you know it needs to be there for at least thirty minutes. It looks pretty good on the outside, but the inside is raw and filled with bacteria. Waiting the extra twenty minutes won't kill you, but impatiently rushing the process might.

Let's take a deeper look at Abraham and Sarah. Abraham is known as the father of faith, so I deeply believe he trusted God's promise that he would become the father of many nations, even though it seemed impossible. Sarah, not so much. I imagine her nagging poor Abraham into submission in order to "help" God fulfill His promise in *her* timing (*Genesis 16:1–15*). Sarah (still Sarai at this point) assumed the situation was impossible. "God must be joking. I'm old as dirt!" That's definitely my translation of that scripture. She convinced (or nagged) her husband to take a shortcut. That's a decision that immediately led to regret as well as some other issues that come along with telling her husband to have a baby with another woman.

I'm sure that in Sarah's mind, that impatient decision was justified. Assuming that human nature hasn't changed too drastically since then, Sarah likely had friends around her that agreed with what she was doing, and they were probably there all along telling her that the promise from God didn't have to involve her. They may have helped to shape the doubt that told her that it was completely illogical to think that she could conceive a child at her age.

It's definitely easy to see Sarah's error when we read the text, but it's different when you are actively experiencing something. Aren't we all at least occasionally guilty of trying to "help" God along with His plans for us because it's taking too long, according to us? Have you ever taken a job because it seemed to make sense, knowing that it was not what God said you would be doing? Have you ever settled into a living situation knowing that God wants better for you? Have you ever done this when God told you to do that? I think that covers everyone.

I've gotten a clear no before, which I tried so hard to push past. There was a point in my young 20s when I had no clue what

I was supposed to be doing. I think that's most young 20-somethings. I decided randomly one day that I would become a nurse. I heard the money was good, and it was a great job for a single mom like I was at the time. So, I dove in. I enrolled in school and started taking classes. I did very well until this ONE class, English. A class that should've been the easiest in the world for me because I had always been great at writing. But I landed with this teacher who scored me lower unless I dumbed down my writing. I got a C, and I had to take the class again due to how competitive the nursing program was at the time. I felt God tell me that I should leave school and that nursing was not what I was supposed to do. I ignored that. I was doing so well that I chose to keep going. I took the class again a year later and landed with the same stinking teacher. This time, I knew what to expect, so I dumbed down everything I wrote and got all As and Bs. I got to my final grade and had a D. What in the world? It turns out she did not submit a lot of my grades. I had to go find my work and bring it to her, only to be missing some of the graded versions myself. I turned in what I could find and I ended up with a 79.8. SERIOUSLY? I got a C AGAIN!

I should add that before I tried going for this, God told me I'd be writing a book and that He had plans for me. I figured I was helping God by setting myself up to have the money and free time to write the book. Or something. Ha! Now God, like the patient father He is, let me go off and be stubborn just to bring me right back to where I needed to be. And with that, school got the boot. Now fast forward to nearly a decade later, and I find it comical that the very subject I just couldn't make the grade in would be what altered my path and become the very thing I am doing to this day. I could've saved some time had I just waited for God to make things happen when He knew they should happen.

God does not need our help. Remember how He set this whole thing up? Remember how He stands outside of time? He literally has all the time in not just the world, but He has all the time in eternity. He knows what He has purposed for you and exactly when it should take place. His timing is often given in such a way that, if the time is used wisely, we can prepare for what He has planned for us. Even if we have no clue at all what that plan may be.

While it is not for us to necessarily make things happen, it is wise to be prepared. Let's say tomorrow you get up and get ready in a hurry. You drive 45 minutes to work. When you get there, you realize you've left everything you need to do your job at home. You can't even get into the building because you've left your access keys and ID badge as well. Now you have to drive all the way back home, figure out where you left everything, and hope you still have a job because it's your first day, and by the time you get back, you'll be about three hours late—here in the Atlanta area, traffic is an all-day thing, you know. But you swore you were ready when you left, remember? Wouldn't it have been better to leave KNOWING you were fully ready? It would be even better if you had someone there helping you to check every detail so that you can be completely ready the first time. Then you won't have to waste time and energy starting over and over again. It's better that once you arrive at your destination, your goals, what God has promised, and what you've been waiting for, you can take hold and never let go because you are equipped to handle it all.

Can you start a job without first going through training? How can you buy a house without saving money or building credit? How can you expect to be a great spouse without learning to be a great friend, sibling, or coworker?

"If you stay ready, you ain't got to get ready." Andy Mineo

That reminds me of the story about the bridesmaids. Only five were smart enough to prepare, and the other five missed the party because they thought they could bum off the other ladies for some lamp oil (Matthew 25:13). The bridesmaids in this parable had no idea what time the bridegroom would show up, but they knew he was coming. He could come at half past eight or maybe at the break of dawn. Only the bridesmaids with enough oil to last through the night were present when the groom arrived.

This is not to say that God won't give any blessings if you don't prepare yourself, but some of His gifts do require a bit of preparation and growth before they can be given. If you want a job that has a bilingual requirement, you don't just show up to the interview speaking only English. You would've already spent the time learning and practicing the other language, so you don't look like a fool being sent out of the interviewer's office after only 60 seconds. If you want to run a 10K, you can't just show up at the starting line and expect to complete the race based solely on your natural awesomeness. As awesome as you are, you must train and condition your body in order to successfully run the race.

If you are in a season of waiting, why not use the time wisely? When I started writing this book, one of my greatest desires was to become a wife. At that moment, I knew that I might not be someone's wife by the next day, but I could work towards being a great wife today while I was given the time. I did this by allowing God to work on me in various areas. I allowed God to build confidence in me during that time so that I would have a greater ability to trust and allow my future husband to be the leader he now is. I wanted to be a wife who would take care of her husband and home, so I went from cooking twice a year to a few times a week. I also worked at keeping a clean home so I would be ready to take care of our home in the future. I asked God to increase my financial wisdom so that my future husband and I could prosper in the future. I took care of my body and my appearance so I could look good for my husband. The list goes on. I did all of this so that I would already be in the habit of doing these things once he arrived. I didn't want to say "I do" and then feel blindsided by all that comes with that commitment, especially with the amount of time I'd been given to prepare. Now that I am a wife, I am so grateful that God allowed me all those years to get myself ready. This by no means made me a perfect wife, but I am much better than I would've been if I had just sat around doing nothing, waiting to be found.

I also love that everything I did to make myself a great wife in the future also helped me to be a greater person while I waited.

Can I also stop for a praise break about God's timing? God knew every lesson that was needed and every bit of growth that needed to happen individually between my husband and me before we could come together. God knew that if even one small detail were off, this would never have happened. It wasn't by chance; it was a divine plan that I'm so thankful for. Waiting for him sucked, but it was most certainly worth every long second. I take this truth with me as I wait for God to come through on some other great desires in my life.

We all have desires that God has placed in us. Take advantage of the time given between conception and realization. If you want God to use you for something, be usable. Pursue the knowledge available. Train yourself in the area that you desire to prosper in. Most of all, use this gift of time (even if you feel like it's more like a curse) to invest in and develop your relationship with Jesus. He knows best which way you should go and what is best for you. Most of all, He knows when.

A huge part of God's timing and getting us prepared is testing.

"Bless our God, O peoples! Give Him a thunderous welcome! Didn't He set us on the road to life? Didn't He keep us out of the ditch? He trained us first, passed us like silver through refining fires. Brought us into hardscrabble country, pushed us to our very limit. Road tested us inside and out, took us to hell and

back. Finally He brought us to this well-watered place." Psalm 66:8-12

Once your faith has reached a certain maturity level, you will more than likely go through various seasons of testing and refining before you can begin to step into the promises and plans God has lined up for you. It will feel unfair at times, but honestly, this is a concept that we all, in and out of the faith, should be used to at this point in life. Testing is simply a natural part of progress.

In every grade, from kindergarten all the way through college, tests are given to assess a student's progress from one topic to another. Tests are given to see if that same student is ready to move on to the next grade level and eventually graduate. Students are refined through daily lessons, studying, and quizzes to improve in areas they previously lacked knowledge in. When the time comes, tests are given to determine if they will move on or if more time is needed to improve or go back and try again.

In order to drive a car legally, we must take a driver's test before we receive a license. When we go looking for a new job, we are tested through the interview process to see if we truly fit the position. Testing is accepted as a normal part of life, but somehow, when it comes to God, we want things to come easy and we want them immediately. Yes, God is completely capable and can make things happen at any point, but for our sake, He generally won't do things that way. God, in His infinite wisdom, knows what we will break or what will break us if given to us at the wrong time and when we aren't prepared.

Let's go back to school for a second. Pop quiz time! Man, I hated those. Had I known there would be a quiz, I would've studied at least a little, right? While we probably all hated those stupid pop quizzes, there is generally no information on that quiz that hadn't been previously taught in class, given as homework, or contained in the textbook. Your grade on that test would reflect one of two things. One: how much had you been paying attention and doing the work that was assigned to you? Two: it will show how you respond to the pressure of being tested, especially in a surprise situation. You may know every answer but still fail if you allow the pressure to take over. Anxiety and the fear of making mistakes will cause you to second-guess everything you know. If you are unprepared, don't pay attention to the knowledge given to you, or simply refuse to take the test, you will fail.

While you're waiting and being tested, remember that God is just asking you to apply what He's already taught you so far. Every message preached, every Bible verse, all the wise counsel I hope you're getting, every song of worship, and every day you live and walk in faith are all part of the lesson plan. You have been given all the tools and knowledge you'll need to succeed and pass any test that comes your way.

The thing is that it is completely up to you. You have to choose to pay attention, study, and do the work. God will not force you to do these things. But how much do you really want the things that you are believing God for? Hopefully, enough to make you want to put in the work to get ready for it all. But again, that's your choice.

If you've done all the groundwork and passed through the refining process, you will be able to walk confidently, knowing that you are far more ready to handle whatever is coming your way. You won't have to wing it, and you won't have to fear not knowing what to do with what you're given. You will know how to handle it and know all the instructions or rules that come with that responsibility. The tests are not meant to break you, but God is ensuring that you are fully ready when the time comes.

CHAPTER 3

STOP BACKSEAT DRIVING

I used to fantasize about my desires. I would fast-forward to the good parts. I'd picture myself in that lovely place with all the people I'm supposed to be with, doing everything I've been hoping to do. But I forgot something. I omitted the journey. It's not often that we get to travel from point A to point B without any curves, detours, or pit stops in between.

Your journey is more like points A–Z, with all the letters in between. A–B may start off nice and smooth. Points C–F could be like taking a stroll through a Category 5 hurricane. G–J might bring some new characters into the mix. The next five points may feel like you're making progress, while the following few make you feel like you're moving backward. Hopefully, you'll realize at some point that you won't be able to figure this out and let God guide you through the unpredictability that takes you to point Z.

"Trust in the Lord with all your heart. Do not depend on your own understanding. Seek His will in all you do, and He will show you what path to take." Proverbs 3:5–6

God sees the big picture. He knows exactly what it will take for you to learn what you need to know to prepare you for your future. He knows your capacity to endure. He knows all that needs to take place in order for you to truly treasure every gift He wants to give to you.

The road you take is often just as important as your destination. You don't learn anything at graduation except maybe some names you've struggled to remember over the past few years. You learned in your classes and through experiences with friends and even enemies. Sure, we'd all like to fast-forward to the end and accept a reward for all the parts we skipped over. All the tests and pop quizzes prove that we know (or don't know) what we should. They show whether or not we are able to graduate to the next level.

Only God knows all the various things that will happen between points A and Z, and He is the only one who can show us which way to go. Trying to navigate without God would be like using a GPS from the year 2002. You WILL get lost. You'll encounter dead ends, get stuck in construction zones, and turn onto roads that no longer exist. God is the perfect GPS. Better than Google Maps and Waze. He assesses all possible routes. The way He told you to go may seem to add miles and minutes compared to the way you would choose on your own. Even if you get confused about the road He told you to take, if you stay on it, you'll learn that He was guiding you around all the traffic, road work, and accidents.

I swear I am guilty of trying to backseat drive with God all the time. Admit it. So are you. "God! You missed the turn!" I sometimes wonder if God takes a moment to shoot a strong side-eye. I'd imagine His response sounding something like this: "My child, my special child. Did I not make this whole place? How on earth could I get lost when I made the earth?" It's something like your kids asking if you're lost when you choose to drive another route. Just recently, my daughter thought I was lying about the destination because I took a route that she had never seen before but that I had driven many times before. If I had taken the route that she was familiar with, the drive would've taken an additional 20 minutes, but at that moment, she thought she knew best. You know how kids are—the same way we are with God. Ha!

You have to decide. Do you go the way you think is faster, or do you trust your GPS? Remember, I said God is the perfect GPS. No glitches. No taking you to the wrong place or not telling you which side of the street you need to be on. 100% reliable 100% of the time. You still have to decide. Do you go your own way?

I do ignore my GPS sometimes. I'll look at the crazy route it gives me, and if I can get a general idea of where I'm going, I'll ignore it and do my own thing. I was only looking to get an estimate on what time I would arrive anyway. I proceed to take the way I feel like going, and then I get stuck in traffic. I end up losing more time than I thought I would lose had I just followed my GPS directions. Ugh!

We do this with God too. He gives us our vision and begins to lead us in the way we should go. But in feeling uncomfortable with the path being laid out for us, we chose to try an existing path that we recognized to get somewhere new. We want what's familiar, or even to be in control of how we get to our destinations. But then we get frustrated when we get stuck in traffic, which slows us down.

I find it funny how we believe that we know how to get somewhere we've never been. If I fly into Paris for the first time today, I cannot get myself to the Eiffel Tower. Even if I saw it from the plane, I would not know what roads to take. I can't read the street signs, and I am not even sure what side of the road I would need to drive on. Without help, I could end up in Belgium. OR, I could humble myself and accept a guide.

Try a little humility. Accept not knowing and be okay with following the One who does. The patience process requires a great amount of humility. I always thought it was funny in old movies and shows when you see a man driving around, and you know he's lost. The wife is usually on the passenger side, yelling at him to stop for directions, but he is either way too confident in his map-reading skills or too proud to admit he hasn't got a clue. Every time, the family would end up somewhere crazy. But life is like that for a lot of us. All we're missing is the ugly station wagon.

"We can make our own plans, but the Lord gives the right answer." Proverbs 16:1

The Holy Spirit may whisper to you to stop and ask for help, but you brush it off because you know what you're doing. Why should you end up lost and out of gas when you have the greatest resource ever? All pride. You could end up embarrassed and disappointed for no good reason. I hope that by the end of this, you will understand that God is right there with you, ready and willing to help. Ready to get you where you need to be. Pride will keep you from asking.

"First pride, then the crash-the bigger the ego, the harder the fall." Proverbs 16:18

I've probably been taken down by pride every time it rears its ugly head. I'll ignore the directions God gave me and try doing my own thing to make the desires HE gave me happen. How does that even work? But it'll seem like I've got what I want in my grasp. Then I fall. I find out that what was in front of me at the moment wasn't for me. Then I experience the pain of that fall, especially if I ran my mouth telling people what was about to be mine and then it's not. Then I'm forced back to square one, a place I shouldn't have left without God in the first place.

I've landed in this position recently at work. I laid out plans for myself to move up, mostly because I felt it was time to move on. I do believe that feeling was from God, but I was on my own in pursuit of my next movement. I applied for multiple positions, all of which I was definitely qualified for. After the fact, I was wise enough to ask God to close any door I wasn't meant to walk through. Guess what? He closed every single one. Even the ones that didn't seem to make sense at the moment. Well, okay then. Later on, I was offered a position at another location. Like I didn't apply or anything; they called and asked me. Without a moment to talk to God, I said yes. Well, that one was taken away.

I definitely placed myself on an unnecessary detour, but God always brings us right where we need to be. Taking a moment to seek God and let Him know I trust His plan and direction in my life has me back on course. He let me know that He has more for me than the position and company I've been content with working at for eight years. Basically, I needed to reposition myself in the passenger seat because my directions were all wrong.

Sometimes we need a good knockdown. It stinks at the moment, but it can cause us to return to a place of humility, face down in front of the One who is bigger than what we want and our pride. I recently went through a major downward spiral, but it led me to remember something I lost along the way. It's not about me. Not even what I want for me is about me. Everything is about God's glory. Everything. It's no wonder why the pause button gets hit on life sometimes. When you're forced to pause or wait, let God guide you back onto the path. Don't worry about the unfamiliar territory you'll have to travel to. Take the time to put your focus back on God so He can lead you. Get in the passenger seat and put your seatbelt on so you will stay in your place.

CHAPTER 4

PRAYER AND PRAISE

Dear God,

I've been waiting a while now. Can you please bless me and end this wait? Amen.

Hey, God, it's me again. I am still waiting. Can you work on that, please? Amen.

God! Hello! Can you hear me up there? Can you please end this wait already? It's taking forever. Amen.

I feel like the longer the wait, the more prayers begin to sound like this. I don't know about you, but there have been many times when I have gotten tired of asking, and my prayers switched back to the generic version I learned when I was a kid. "Thank you, God, for this and that. Bless my family and me. I pray for a good day. Amen." That is not okay. Not when you have barriers to break through. Not when you have mountains to climb. Not when you have territories to conquer.

Prayer is major. It is both the greatest weapon and the greatest tool. It can destroy what needs to be destroyed and build what needs to be built. Prayer is the only weapon that works in both the spiritual and natural realms. It is the best thing to do while waiting for anything. Prayer changes things, even if it just changes your heart and perspective. Prayer keeps you connected to the One who can make anything happen.

Whether or not we agree with the outcome, prayer always changes things. I know we get tired of always asking, but the Bible has a lot to say about persistent prayer. Luke 11:5-8 shows Jesus telling a story about a friend asking for bread with shameless persistence. If the friend gave up, he would still be hungry, along with his guests. But he kept knocking and received what he came for. *"And so I tell you, keep on asking and you will receive what you ask for. Keep on seeking and you will find. Keep on knocking and the door will be opened to you. For everyone who asks receives. Everyone who seeks finds. And everyone who knocks, the door will be opened"* (Luke 11:9-19).

Keep asking. It's okay. God is not tired of hearing from you.

What I do suggest is that you broaden your prayers to more than "Give me, amen." Pray over your wait. Pray that God reveals any dark areas that need some light. Pray that your faith will grow and carry you through the wait. Ask for wisdom and a clear vision. Pray for what you're praying for.

If it's a spouse, pray for their character, faith, and growth. If it's a career, pray for each boss, trainer, or future coworker. If it's a journey or mission, pray over the destination and the people you will encounter. Pray over the people who will be affected by you and the blessing you're waiting for. Pray for receptive hearts. Pray for favor and that every new door that you'll need to go through will be opened. Pray for your finances, along with the finances of anyone else involved. The best of all is to pray that God's will be done, even if it results in a closed door that will lead you to the right door.

Just pray without ceasing. It is the only way for you to win your battle. You can't show up to a battlefield empty-handed. You'll be crushed. We must show up ready to fight and leave the white flag behind. There is so much we can't see behind the scenes. We have no idea how our prayers are knocking out the resistance.

I'll take it up another level and add fasting to the mix. Whether it's a Daniel fast, a total fast, or just fasting from distractions, turning that hunger into prayer makes things happen in the spirit like nothing else can. Daniel 10 shows us why we must push on and what happened when Daniel fasted.

"Since the first day you began to pray for understanding and to humble yourself before your God, your request has been heard in heaven. But for 21 days the spirit prince of Persia blocked my way. Then Michael, one of the archangels, came to help me, and I left him there with the spirit prince of the kingdom Persia." Daniel 10:12-13

Because of Daniel's prayers and fasting, God sent warriors to him to fight the things he couldn't see. I say warriors because it helps me see angels for what they really are—big, strong warriors. I'm not sure where we got the image of cute, naked babies or some docile character with wings and a halo, because anytime you see an angel show up in the Bible, they had people on their knees in fear. That's who I want you to see fighting your spiritual battles.

You may need 21 days of fasting and prayer like Daniel, or you may need a week. Either way, you are making sure those warriors are being sent your way, pushing through the spirit of fear and any other demons you may be dealing with. They can lay down spirits sent your way by others around you, and they can slay those spirits that intend to keep you down and keep you from getting to where God has called you to be. You're waiting anyway, so you have the space to be committed to persistent prayer. Every prayer gets you one step closer to the goal. More importantly, each prayer strengthens your bond with the person you're talking to. Jesus. That bond eases that wait time like nothing else can.

I know that simply saying "pray" does not come easy to everybody. So many people have problems connecting with God in prayer. Many of us were trained to believe that prayer should look or sound a certain way, like if I don't go into my prayer closet for hours, God won't hear me. Or if I don't pray like the people do at church and say my words a certain way, God won't listen. I'm glad I learned that lesson because I am a girl who prays and gets distracted easily. Thank God for telling us to strive for relationships over religion. God already knows you and what's in your heart. He knows what you are waiting for and what you are going through. He just wants you to come to Him as your true self and tell Him all about it. Talk to Him genuinely, and He will listen. Tell Him the desires of your heart and ask Him for what you are longing for. He asked us to pray without ceasing (1 Thessalonians 5:17). You are not bugging God. You are free to keep asking. It just so happens that one of the ways I talk to and listen to God is by writing. It forces me to keep my mind on task. God made you with a special way to connect to Him. I'll dig into that in just a few moments. Just tap in and ask away.

"Keep on asking, and you will receive what you ask for. Keep on seeking and you will find. Keep on knocking and the door will be opened." Matthew 7:7-8

Now there is context to this scripture, of course. God is not a genie present just to grant your every wish. We must stop behaving like spoiled children, saying, "I want it my way, and I want it now!" and then having full-on meltdowns when God responds to our request like the perfect parent He is. He will never give us more than we can handle or anything that is not good for us.

Just as there is no formula for how we should pray, there is also no formula for how God will answer our prayers. But I promise He always answers. If what you're asking isn't in God's will for you, He can and will say no. If God sees that what you're asking for will hurt you, the answer is no. If He sees that you or what you're praying for are not ready, He will say not right now (try not to confuse that one with a no). It's far too common for people to treat the no's and maybes as God ignoring their prayers when, in reality, they are just ignoring or don't like the answer.

Sometimes God's answer comes by way of His switching things up. You may pray that God should give you a certain job. He may answer by letting a company pass on you but then arranging a meeting between you and a critical person. You're then sent in a completely different direction, one that takes you not only to what you have been waiting for but does it in a way you've never imagined and bigger than you've ever dreamed.

Stay on guard in this area. The enemy will try to take you out of the game by attempting to kill your prayer life. I can say firsthand how your prayers can start dying out when things seem to be taking forever, or you feel like those prayers you've been praying for years seem to go unanswered. The enemy will try to whisper in your ear, "God isn't listening." LIE!!! That one lie may have you turning back to generic rhetorical prayers: "Thank you for today, God. Bless me, give me something, and goodnight." Or it'll be a day of prayer missed here, which can easily snowball into days, weeks, and even months without speaking to God. You will have dropped the biggest and most powerful weapon you need for this fight and any others yet to come. Don't do it.

"Don't be afraid, Daniel. Since the first day you began to pray for understanding and to humble yourself before your God, your request has been heard in heaven. I have come in answer to your prayer. But for twenty-one days the spirit prince of the kingdom of Persia blocked my way." Daniel 10:12-13

Hold on to the hope that God has already sent His messengers to strengthen you along the way as you wait for Him to answer your prayers. Keep on praying through the waiting. Pray for endurance so you don't give up or settle for less. Pray for more faith so you will continue to believe that what God told you is indeed true. Ask for wisdom and discernment so you know what is from God and what is a distraction. Pray for relationships that will encourage and help you now and once you walk in what God has for you. Just keep praying. I promise He hears you.

We must become extremely sensitive to the sound of our Father's voice and be aware of imitations and distractions. I hear many Christians say they have a hard time hearing God or that they believe He doesn't speak to them at all. The problem is that many of us, at some point or another, have humanized how we think we should hear God's voice. We're looking for the movie version, which involves either hearing a big, booming voice or having a Morgan Freeman-type character appear in a white suit and give us some direct guidance. It sounds nice, but no. God created us uniquely, so it should be no surprise that the way He speaks to each of us is tailored to that uniqueness. If you're waiting for God to yell out, "Hey, it's me, God! I have something to tell you!" You will miss it.

"Go out and stand before me on the mountain," the Lord told him. And as the Lord passed by, a mighty windstorm hit the mountain. It was such a terrible blast that the rocks were torn loose, but the Lord was not in the wind. After the wind, there was an earthquake, but the Lord was not in the earthquake. And after the earthquake there was a fire. But the Lord was not in the fire. And after the fire, there was a sound of a gentle whisper. When Elijah heard it, he wrapped his face in his cloak and went out and stood at the entrance of the cave." 1 Kings 19:11–13

When God communicates with us, it's rarely big or obvious. So often, we want God to give us a burning bush or a flashing sign with specific directions. You may be waiting a long time for that one. As we move in patience during the waiting seasons, we each have to lean in and pay attention. Picture yourself in a room full of people. There's music playing or a TV playing an action movie. Your best friend is there and has something important they need to tell you. Your friend begins to speak softly to you. Of course, you can't hear, so you back away from the noise and lean in to hear what your friend has to say, and the words are whispered directly into your ears. Rather than asking God to turn the volume up on His voice, try turning down the competing noise and leaning in so you can hear the whisper.

I swear, the longer we wait, the more it feels like God isn't saying anything. Trust me, He is speaking. It just may "sound" different than what you expected. There is no generic formula. Going into a prayer closet and having meditation time sounds nice. It works for some people. Lord knows how many times I've tried that approach and failed. That was me doing what all the old Christian ladies told me I should do. I even tried getting on my knees and getting under a prayer cloth. Super not for me. I don't know how your mind works, but mine is a wanderer and always going a mile a minute, so sitting still and in silence doesn't work for me. I just end up fighting with the randomness of my mind as I try to stay on track or fall asleep. Either way, I've accomplished nothing.

If you're struggling to hear God, there's this great thing He gave us with all sorts of speaking in it. The Bible. It has hundreds of pages of God's voice. Seeing His words helps us understand His heart and get to know Him a bit. Those scriptures will help us determine when God is speaking to us or when it is coming from somewhere else. We need that deciphering tool because God will not be the only one speaking, and He will not be the loudest one in the room.

I learned quickly that I hear God when I write. Do you think I would've had any of these words to put down on paper without Him? Many days I pick up a pen and have no idea what I am about to write and am not even in the mood to write. Yes, I'm old school and prefer the organic nature of writing with an actual pen in cursive on paper. God always takes over, and then I end up with a lesson on paper. I hear from God at church, through other people, in books, in dreams, in movie themes, etc., and the Bible helps me to weed out the fact that the devil can talk to you in all of these ways too.

God speaks differently based on maturity, the season you're in, and your waiting times, and it's always in a way that's specific to the person and the moment. Someone newer to the faith will be taught and spoken to, like a parent teaching their child how to ride a bike. For the first few times, your dad will hold on and run alongside you as you learn to balance. Then he'll start to let go a little as he stays next to you ready to catch you when you start to wobble. But at some point, dad has to let go. He will be present when you need him, but he knows he doesn't have to be there every second because you've got this. Hearing from God is just like this. When faith in God is new and fresh, you often see and hear God in everything. Prayers seem to be answered instantly. I remember once having a prayer answered the moment I thought about it. I was a newborn in the faith, so I needed that constant care. But as I grew in my faith, patience had to set in. I experienced a lot more "no" and "not yet" responses. My faith was strong enough for the delays, and it was time for my character and endurance to grow.

"We can rejoice, too, when we run into problems and trials, for we know that they help us develop endurance. And endurance develops strength of character, and character strengthens our confident hope of salvation. And this hope will not lead to disappointment. For we know how dearly God loves us, because he has given us the Holy Spirit to fill our hearts with His love." Romans 5:1-5

Keep on praying. Pray like your life depends on it. Pray like it's the fuel that gets the engine of your dreams going. Then, when you feel like you're all prayed out or are unsure what to pray for, begin to praise Him. Praise Him for all He's done and because He's not done with you yet.

"Let the godly sing for joy to the Lord. It is fitting for the pure to praise Him. Praise the Lord with melodies on the lyre; make music for Him on the harp, and sing with joy. For the word of the Lord holds true, and we can trust everything He does."
Psalms 33:1-4

Praise shifts our focus and softens our hearts. It puts our focus back where it should be—on Jesus. David sang praises throughout the Psalms. The crazy thing is that many of those psalms were written while he was on the run, living in caves and fighting for his life, all while waiting for God to save him and restore his position as king. David is a great example of how to praise God in the best of times and the worst of times. He grasped something we all need to understand: God is sovereign and good even when the wait feels eternal or when your world seems to be crumbling around you.

I can think of a number of occasions when my waiting has left me discouraged, and I thank God for worship, especially at church when everyone is joined together in praise. During the times that I didn't feel I had it in me to praise on my own, a room filled with the Spirit would draw me in, take me out of myself, and cause me to look back to God. A time like when I was 30 years old and felt completely stuck. Feeling like I would never be able to move out of my parents' house. When I felt so full of purpose but had no clue when I'd be released to move in it. I felt completely overlooked and like there was no way I'd ever get married. And honestly, so much more lies in the land of inadequacies. In those times, I couldn't find comfort in anyone. But in worship, singing songs about the goodness of my Father, I received comfort. In those moments of worship, even alone in my car, I could cry out words through song that gave me the strength to push on, and my hopes were revived.

It's easy to get sucked into circumstances, but praising helps us remember all that God has already done. Then we are more confident in the things that He is doing now that we aren't even aware of. Praise God for what He's done. Praise God for what He is doing. Praise God for what He will do. Praise God for those bullets He made you dodge. We want God to give us so much that the least we can do is to pause the asking and, in praise, appreciate all that He's already given.

Then that praise will circle back and strengthen your prayers. It's like adding fuel as a boost to get your prayers on track. Your prayers will shift from a place of desperation and hopelessness to a place of peace and hope. Your faith will be lifted because you will remind yourself of the One holding it all together and of every single time God has come through for you already.

Being surrounded by praise can revive your heart even more. The church I attend periodically holds worship services, and let me tell you something. There is nothing like it. It's not specifically about the songs, or who is singing that week, or the sound system, or any other theatrics. It is all about being surrounded by other believers as you cover yourself in songs filled with the truth of God's word. You will experience, and see all around you, various kinds of healing. Sometimes it's physical. Sometimes it's mental. But most of all, in faith, spiritual healing and revival are there for all.

You may not always know what to pray about in a moment. I know I've experienced times of being so all-around drained that I had no idea what to pray for. But I could still sing. And those songs could become my prayers. I could use those songs to speak life into the areas of myself that seemed dead. In both prayer and praise, we can be reminded of something so simple. God never left. We may have gone adrift, but God is always there every time we choose to seek Him. I love that about Him.

CHAPTER 5

THE GRASS IS GREENER ON THE OTHER SIDE... SO THEY SAY

The grass is greener on the other side. Have you ever come across a person who just seems to have it all together? This person is attractive and has a great body. They work in an impressive industry, might drive a nice car, and have an amazing home on the best side of town. They are married, of course, with super smart kids. 401K on point, always present to serve the community, all while appearing to be well rested. They have it all. While you may be happy for this person, you occasionally look at what you're doing and feel a bit lacking. You're cute, but you feel like you could visit the gym a little more. Your job is decent, but it's still a fight to make ends meet sometimes. Looking at them makes your life feel a little subpar. What do you gain from this line of thinking?

"Comparison is the thief of contentment." It is also a horrible, treacherous killer of patience and peace. It can snatch us right out of an otherwise joyful time and leave us feeling anxious about things we don't yet have. I think we all fall victim to this from time to time, more so when we see those around us granted things so easily (or so it seems) while we are working so hard for the same things.

Imagine seeing a coworker get promoted after only a year in the same position you've been in for five years. Or seeing someone you know getting married after what seemed like 5 minutes of dating while you've been waiting for years. How about when you see that person who started going to the gym a few months ago achieving amazing results while you have been struggling to see your own progress? Blah, blah, blah. The grass is always greener on the other side, right? I bet the grass is greener because the person who owns it decided to focus on and take care of their own grass without worrying so much about what was on the other side of the fence. These things are part of those people's stories. You have no idea what their struggles are, how hard they have worked, or what God's purpose is for them. It's time to get back to watering your own grass.

If you're always staring over the fence at the neighbor's grass, who is tending to yours? The crazy thing is, you may not even have the same type of grass as your neighbor. Yours may require different soil. It may need to be fertilized with something special. You may need to water it more frequently. Who knows, but at the beginning, middle, and end of the day, that is your grass.

Clearly, God has alternative plans for you. We are not all meant to receive the same blessings at the same time as everyone else. We don't have a cookie-cutter God, so we don't get cookie-cutter stories. We don't all go to school, land a dream job, get married, have 2.5 kids (however you do that), and live happily ever after. That sounds more like a 1960s sitcom than real life.

It's extremely likely that the person you are comparing yourself to is someone you would not trade places with if given the opportunity. This could be for a few reasons. Their tailor-made struggle may be something you would not have been able to persist in. All the exact pieces of the puzzle had to get them where they are, just the same as you, and if even one small detail were different, it would not even be the same person. In that same line of thinking, I can bet there are parts of your life and your story that made you who you are and that you wouldn't trade for the world. A huge reason, especially in this day and age, is that it may all be plastic. It's all a show to make them look great to the outside world, and it will all fall apart if even a small thread is pulled. No matter the reason, you can never compete with being the next person.

We were each created uniquely, with unique desires, unique gifts, a unique purpose, and a unique journey. Shouldn't our lives play out in such a way that God gets the glory rather than impressing those looking at us? Are the desires of our heart simply for our own benefit, or are they part of a greater plan?

It's unfair for you to compare yourself to what someone else is doing. It halts you from walking in your own purpose and inhibits you from being the best you. Running around trying to be like someone else will always leave you in second place. You'll often end up stepping out of God's will and right into your own. All you will accomplish is delaying the process and getting mad at God because He's taking too long. Why attempt to be a second-rate someone else when you can always be the number-one you?

"Pay attention to your own work, for you will get the satisfaction of a job well done, and you won't need to compare yourself to anyone else. For we are all responsible for our own conduct." Galatians 6:4–5

Better efforts should be placed on chasing the desires God placed in you rather than what your friend, brother, coworker, or that person on Instagram is doing. If you must compare, only compare yourself with the person you were yesterday and the person you want to be tomorrow. Then don't forget to match it all up with Jesus because, while it's not okay to compare, it is perfectly fine and encouraged for you to follow a great example.

"Look straight ahead, and fix your eyes on what lies before you. Mark out a straight path for your feet; stay on the safe path." Proverbs 4:25–26

What a great thing it is to focus on and succeed at your own work—no looking left or right—just focusing on what God laid out for you. Then, when you finish, you can take pride in what you've done and what God has done through you. God gets the glory. If you try to be like someone else, no matter how well you do, you'll be viewed as a copycat, and there is not the same level of joy in completing something already done by someone else.

Stay focused on your own road, and you will make it where you need to be in due time. Have you ever tried to drive your car by only staring at the cars in your side mirrors? Don't. You will crash. If you spend your life focused on what others are doing rather than on your own walk, you will crash. So, look up and trust the One who is paving the road for you.

Now, if you're good about keeping your eyes focused, make sure you protect your ears. I don't mean putting on ear muffs to keep them warm. But the people around you will have a lot to say about your choice to wait for the desires God has placed in you. This is when you have to tell other people to stop worrying about your grass and mind their own.

Don't let the words and opinions of others lead you to believe that waiting for what God has promised you is crazy. When God tells you very clearly what you are waiting for, you will no doubt have to become a master at ignoring some people. This may even include those with good intentions. Sometimes God will give you a vision, and you may be the only one who gets to know about it for a time. Maybe a few will understand when you share, and they will support your choice, but there are others who will think you're pretty much nuts, much like when an angel told Zechariah that he and his wife would soon have a son named John. He and Elizabeth knew God had given this name to their son, yet everyone else combatted Elizabeth's decision, and Zechariah could not speak to back her up (Luke 1:11–21; 59–64).

You will almost always go against the grain with Jesus in this life. Even more so when you are willing to wait any length of time or by any means to receive what God has promised you because you know what He says will be.

"As the rain and the snow come down from heaven, and do not return to it without watering the earth and making it bud and flourish, so that it yields seed for the sower and bread for the eater, so is my word that goes out from my mouth. It will not return to me empty, but will accomplish what I desire and achieve the purpose for which I sent it." Isaiah 55:10–11

In a few seasons of me waiting, I just loved hearing people say, "You're too picky." It's like people are hardwired to have you settle for less when you've passed whatever time they find acceptable for waiting. It's bizarre to them that you won't just give in to any option thrown your way. I prefer not to be like the first round of Israelites, who saw God move in great power for them but still ended up settling for a nonsense idol in the form of a gold cow because they didn't know how long it would take for Moses to come down from the mountain and lead them into the promised land. Because of their impatience and stupidity, these people wandered the desert for 40 years until that generation died off, and God passed the promise on to their children. They missed out because of impatience and unbelief. I would much rather wait 40 days in silence than roam for 40 years and never make it to my destination.

Other people often have no clue what is promised to you or what all that entails, and they will not entirely comprehend why you are willing to wait for those promises. Even if you try to explain, they may still be lost. You may even have someone tell you that if you take things into your own hands, the promise may be yours that way. But again, remember how that worked out for Sarah, Abraham, and Hagar (Genesis 16). My most fun times were when friends would tell me that I needed to put myself out there if I wanted to be found by a husband. They missed the whole "being found" part. They told me there was no way my husband would meet me if I never left my couch. The joke was on them because that's exactly where I was when I reconnected with my now-husband.

No one has the authority to label your patient obedience as pickiness, stubbornness, or even foolishness. It is okay to not date the guy or girl who shows you interest just because that is the first person to come along in a long time and everyone in your circle says you should just do it. It's okay to not accept the mediocre job just because it is offered to you. It's okay to stick to your convictions when you know that God is in it and is watching carefully over your current, yet temporary, situation.

I strongly encourage you to shut down those labels and any discouraging conversations in their tracks. Dismiss the negative thoughts that will likely accompany those things. If it is God's promise or desire, then these people are actually calling God too picky. Try not to take it too personally. Is God being too picky by wanting the best for you and knowing exactly what you need and when? I'm sure we'd all prefer God to be picky rather than sending us nonsense just for time's sake.

CHAPTER 6

CHECK THE SOURCE

For a time, I begged God to allow me to move out on my own. Initially, it was simply because I wanted my own space. I wanted to be able to come home and not have to talk to anyone. I wanted to be able to leave a dish in the sink until morning. I wanted my own bubble; one I could stay in with just me and my daughter. As long as that was the thought, I went nowhere. Somewhere along the lines, God changed my heart and let me know that the desire for my own space was good, but the motive was not so much. Down the line, the reasons changed. I wanted space to entertain freely with no time limits. I wanted to offer a place for my friends to experience peace if they needed it. I wanted a place for children to come and not worry about breaking anything. And, of course, I wanted my daughter to have the best education I could give her. When my motive changed, God blessed me tremendously, far beyond what I thought I could have.

Desires should be checked often, and their roots need to be examined. There are God-given and God-approved desires, and then there are others that you'll form on your own based on other factors. From the very start of life, we are given the formula for how we should live. It comes by way of children's fairy tales with happy endings. All sorts of books, shows, magazines, social media posts, and movies portray the perfect outcome. These desires are even formed by notions of how life should be lived that have been passed down from one generation to the next.

Society, family, and they (whoever they are) say life should happen in a specific order: school, career, marriage, kids, and then you'll be happy. as long as you do all these things before you turn 27. By 30, you are supposed to have accomplished it all. Flourishing career. Homeowner status. Your house is always magazine-perfect, and your kids are perfectly behaved geniuses. Somewhere, somehow, many of us have found it completely acceptable to form our own desires around this line of thinking. All these things we are all supposed to have and fight to obtain These cookie-cutter expectations only crush us when we don't meet them on time and get frustrated at God for not making it all happen.

Is life really supposed to look so much like Pleasantville? That movie where everyone was the same and everything was black and white, and deviation was not allowed. We just end up with all this anxiety for no real reason. There are way too many pity parties thrown for 30th birthdays because all these boxes have not been checked off by then.

Who says? Did God put those weights on you, or are you being enticed to try to live a life that was not meant for you? Did you go into prayer, and God showed you this picket fence revelation? I strongly doubt it. Nowhere in the Bible have I ever seen God handing out duplicate visions and journeys. God shares His vision with us to try to keep us from being tempted to live the way the world says we should.

"No temptation has overtaken you except what is common to mankind. And God is faithful; He will not let you be tempted beyond what you can bear. But when you are tempted, He will also provide a way out so that you can endure it." 1 Corinthians 10:13

My walk has definitely not followed the rules at all, despite my best efforts. I guess that makes me a bit of a rebel. I went to college like I was supposed to right after high school. And that's the end of things going according to plan for me. I had my daughter at 19. I left college and worked for minimum wage. I went back to college for nursing because I heard it was great money for a single mom. God said no to that idea, so I left school again with no degree. I worked at a few underwhelming positions before somehow landing in banking. I didn't move out of my parents' house until I was 31. Oh, and I didn't get married until I was 32. According to all the "supposed to's," I've failed at life, and way too many times, I've believed that lie.

But God. I'm right where He wants me. That vague overview of about 15 years doesn't tell you much, but I can tell you that

God's hand has been in every part of it all. He's been guiding me this whole time, whether I was listening to Him or not. And He has completely shaken up what I want in this life, along with why I want it.

God gave me the biggest blessing even in my sin, knowing that my daughter's life would lead me back to Him. I won't even get into the things I desired before that. He told me to leave college so I could focus on being a better mother and free my time to begin serving Him in my church. On top of that, He let me leave school debt-free. Those odd jobs I worked, which seemed meaningless at the time, put me in a position to lead quite a few people to Jesus. Not being able to move out allowed my daughter and I to do some pretty amazing things together. And because I didn't have any big financial strains, it was easy to help the people around me and even some strangers.

What does any of this have to do with patience? Everything. As I waited and still wait for God to come through on what I consider to be my major desires, He has and is continuing to build my character. He has shown me that He can use me in some pretty cool ways even while I'm waiting. It would do me absolutely no good to have a life I think I'm "supposed to" have just handed to me.

"We can rejoice too when we run into problems and trials, for we know that they help us to develop endurance. And endurance develops strength of character, and character strengthens our confident hope of salvation. And this hope will

not lead to disappointment. For we know how dearly God loves us, because He has given us the Holy Spirit to fill our hearts with His love." Romans 5:3–5

Let your unique path to your promise mold and develop you. Thank God for not being boring by having us all do things the same way. The life He has given is about far more than obtaining degrees, status, and money. Let the things that drive you, or you desire to be, complete God's work in your life so that you may be used for a greater purpose.

If all these "supposed to's" are all you're waiting for, what happens if you gain them? Having all the right things for all the wrong reasons will leave you with a void in your life, and you'll never feel like you have enough. These picture-perfect desires can suck us in and even overshadow the vision that God has given us. But only what God gives can truly satisfy. So, throw out all those unfit life goals that don't fit the plan that God has for you. Stay the course and don't allow yourself to be made to feel less than or like a failure because you chose to wait on God's promises for your life rather than trying to live up to some generic expectations. I'd much rather fail in the eyes of society than miss out on what God has up His sleeve for me.

While we are checking our motives, we also need to make sure we're praying for the right things. Sometimes I feel like I'm asking God for the same thing over and over. God knows, and He doesn't suffer from memory loss. But I think He just wants me to pray and not beg. In all the times of pleading prayers, I should've been asking God to increase my wisdom. I'm sure

Solomon showed up every human ever when he made his infamous request to God.

To have God be pleased with me and my prayers to Him is a good enough reason for me to want to refocus my prayers from just a typical petition. When we get into that place of pleasing God, He always goes far above and beyond what we're asking.

At times, it feels like the same thing is being asked for over and over. It starts to feel like nothing is ever going to happen. God knows I have felt that way. Then it hit me one day, and by "hit me," I mean being preached in a church service, reinforced in one of my Bible App plans, and then brought up in a conversation with friends. It turns out that I was asking the wrong question. I've already come to God with my wants and needs. He knows. I mean, like, He really knows because I've been asking for some things for years.

God doesn't suffer from memory loss, so I know if I stop begging, He won't forget. What I should've been asking for all along was for God to increase my wisdom. We should all take the Solomon approach in this area.

"At Gibeon the Lord appeared to Solomon during the night in a dream and God said, 'Ask for whatever you want me to give you.'" 1 Kings 3:5

God knew the heart of who He was talking to, because I'm sure the rest of us would immediately pull out a list of selfish desires. Maybe we would ask for a few things for a few close family members and friends, but it would probably go something like this: "Ok, God, I need money. Like, go on and permanently knock out all these bills, please. I need a husband/wife. Give us some babies. Can I throw in some paid vacations? Heal me and all of my people. Bless me. Bless my family and friends. Bless my church," and so on. So "my" small circle would be blessed and taken care of, but that's about it.

Solomon did things a little differently. He immediately checked himself.

"But I am only a little child and do not know how to carry out my duties." 1 Kings 3:7

Solomon first humbled himself and really assessed where he stood at that moment and what his capabilities without God were before continuing to make his request.

"So give your servant a discerning heart to govern your people and to distinguish between right and wrong. For who is able to govern this great people of yours?"

This guy literally has the world at his fingertips, and all he wants is wisdom? What? That's genius on so many levels. The right wisdom has the ability to take you anywhere. Wisdom teaches investors which stocks will get them the best return for their money. It teaches those in real estate investment exactly when to buy or sell property for the best profit. Wisdom guides parents to know which schools and afterschool programs will best set up their children for success. It can teach people how to spend properly, save money, and increase their credit scores. The possibilities are endless.

Wouldn't it be amazing to have the wisdom needed to make your dream or desire happen for you? Imagine having a beautiful gift placed in your hands. This gift you knew was coming but had no idea when. Wisdom is like getting the instruction manual long before you receive the gift and studying it as much as possible so that when you receive that gift, you can dive right in. No winging it. You've already read the manual and know exactly what to do and how all the parts function. That is what praying for wisdom looks like. You save yourself from having to bump your head and figure things out the hard way as you go.

We should give the Solomon approach a try, aiming for wisdom that benefits more than just me, myself, and mine. The wisdom you ask for could possibly have positive effects that reach far beyond your small circle of friends and family. Most of all, this kind of selfless prayer is pleasing to God. *" The Lord was pleased that Solomon had asked for this" (1 Kings 3:10).*

To have God be pleased would be enough for me, but the God we serve is always going far beyond our limited asking. *So God said to him, "Since you have asked for this and not for long life or wealth for yourself, nor have you asked for the death of your enemies but for discernment in administering justice, I will do what you have asked. I will give you a wise and discerning heart so that there will never have been anyone like you nor will there ever be. Moreover, I will give you what you have not asked for—both wealth and honor so that in your lifetime you will have no equal among kings. And if you walk in obedience to me and keep my commands as David your father did, I will give you a long life" (1 Kings 3:11–14).*

Just look at how God responds to humility and selflessness. Our God always responds above and beyond what we can imagine. The heart of what Solomon was asking was pure. God's response was to give him exactly what he asked for and then level it up by adding all the bells and whistles and added bonuses. That's not only great motivation to check the motive behind my requests to God, but it also gives me hope to keep on waiting for God to come through in response to those prayers.

But who will benefit from God answering your prayers? If the answer is me and mine, it may have to be sent to the fire for refining. Solomon's prayer benefited an entire kingdom, and we are still learning from him as a result of it today. The years I spent praying for a husband were not simply so I could have a companion and someone to make babies with. Those parts are good and dandy, but they are not enough. I also prayed that our marriage would lead people to Jesus. I constantly pray that our children are arrows and will also be major warriors for the kingdom. I pray for wisdom in so many areas, not so I can keep it to myself to grow and increase myself, but I want to share every little bit I get from God with others. It's all way too good to keep to myself.

Prayers for wisdom and discernment have the ability to benefit all who come in contact with the person who prayed, even more than that person alone. A person filled with wisdom tends to delight in sharing with others, and discernment will show them when it's appropriate to share and with whom it will be received. Praying for wisdom in your season of waiting will help you succeed in handling all of the blessings God will send your way and will help you to honor the Giver above His gifts.

God knows you're waiting, but maybe He's waiting for your heart to change. I can appreciate the fact that God chose to speak to Solomon in his dreams. God chose to have a conversation directly with his spirit rather than with his flesh. God spoke straight into Solomon's heart, and as a result, Solomon gave the unfiltered truth. Solomon wasn't able to give a "best behavior" response as his flesh and human reasoning weren't able to get in the way. I can't say my response would be the same, as I still struggle with wanting my selfish desires over what God has planned for me.

The real challenge here is to fix our hearts on kingdom business so the motives behind our desires and requests are pure and align with what God wants for us. When we get our desires, and our hearts are in submission to God's desires for us, God can begin to move freely and completely in our lives. We can see how God gave Solomon things he didn't even ask for because his heart was in the right place. God loves you as much as He loved Solomon, so I know He is more than pleased to add to your life beyond your requests, especially when you approach Him in humility. Maybe it won't be a whole kingdom with extreme riches, but He will send blessings uniquely crafted just for you because He loves you personally. Ask God for the wisdom and discernment you will need to successfully manage all you have been waiting for.

Do you see the way God responds to humility and selflessness? Our God always levels way up in His response to us far beyond what we could think up. That's more than enough reason for me to check the motive behind what I'm asking God to give.

CHAPTER 7

HOPE

God came through and gave you this awesome vision for things to come in your life. He said it would be done in your lifetime. What He told you was something you may have never imagined on your own. "Yes, God! I receive that!" Your spirit and your hopes are sky-high. That breakthrough is right around the corner, or so you thought. Then you realize God never actually told you which corner it would be around.

I can still remember the first time I received a prophecy about my marriage back in 2012. That prophecy was followed by a few dreams, visions, and a stream of prophecies that all seemed to line up over the next few years. There were so many days when I felt like it was never going to happen for me. My hopes would just plummet from time to time, and I would end up in a dark place filled with loneliness, anxiety, and deep sadness. But then I would hear God ask, "Do you trust me?" Then I gradually pushed myself to keep on enduring and keep on hoping even when I couldn't see anything happening. I had no idea it would take until 2019 for that promise to unfold, but in God's timing, it did.

There are times when God tells you something is coming, and it does happen right away, but other times it may take years. I feel there are several reasons for God's timing, as He never says or does anything in vain. I believe we get those instant blessings to give us something to look back on. We can see that God is able and will come through, and that He has the ability to give us the strength we need to push through the long waiting seasons. Major and really life-changing promises usually take more time than short-term goals like needing a bill paid or encouragement. You'll often have to face a few struggles along the way. While seemingly horrible in the moment, those struggles will prepare you and train you to handle what you will receive. I don't like giving the devil too much credit, but he does like to send his goons to try to snatch us off track, especially when he knows the goodness of God is about to happen majorly in your life. Those goons will come in the form of doubt, fear, questioning, and temptation to try to distract you from what's ahead of you. We have to be ready to fight to maintain hope, no matter the delays or deterrents.

"We were given this hope when we were saved. If we already have something, we don't need to hope for it. But if we look forward to something we don't yet have, we must wait patiently and confidently." Romans 8:24–25

Wait patiently and confidently. I know this is easier said than done. Isn't what you're waiting for worth the effort, or at least a bit of hope? When we remember how big our God is—and I mean really think about that—we will be comforted and revived. He can certainly be trusted with all of our hopes and desires.

If you're having a hard time remembering His strength, His power, His grace, His love, or His magnitude, just think about what He has already done in your life. When I read through the Old Testament, I feel like God should've wiped out all those people a few times. How could they forget about Him parting the Red Sea and freeing them from their captors? How could they forget that God gave this child, David, the strength and confidence to take out Goliath? God literally guided them with a pillar of cloud and fire. How could they be so oblivious? They were there! They saw these things with their own eyes! How could they lose hope after only a few days just because their leader was talking to God on a mountain they knew God was on? But wait. I've done the same thing. I went through a season of extreme financial deficit. Single mom with no child support making $150 per week (was very thankful to be living with the parents then). I recall a day when I was looking at a $200 bill with no clue as to how I would pay it. I didn't want to ask my parents because money was tight on their end as well, and they were already providing a roof over my head and so much more. I get a call from my grandmother. She said that the Holy Spirit told her I needed $200. What? Another day, I had to pay $60 for a class my daughter was in. Again, I had no clue where that money was coming from. Then a friend bought a stereo I was selling for $20, but he gave me $60. And God came through like that over and over again, eventually blessing me with a much better job; this is also a testament to why it's good to tithe, but that's a story for another day.

But just like the Israelites, I forget when something new comes up or when the wait just keeps going. I've allowed myself to fall into hopelessness, even though I have personal proof that God is faithful. I'm certain that, if you're honest, you've behaved like the Old Testament crew and have allowed God's past come-throughs to slip your mind. If you're breathing, walking, or have eyes with the ability to read these words or ears to listen, God has already parted many seas to get you to where you are today. He has taken out giants for you. He has and will continue to make a way out of no way for you. Remember these things and keep hoping as long as it takes.

Trust me; I know that hope can be hard to hold on to as the clock ticks on. It's really easy to begin to feel overlooked or forgotten about. Running through day-to-day life, just waiting for a door, a window, or even a crack in the wall to appear so you can start walking into where God promised you would be. It's daunting sometimes. I've been hearing a lot of people speak lately about when they received a revelation from God about plans in their lives, but in that, I've also heard the part when they would say it came to pass 10, 15, or 20 years later. My mind always goes to, "How in the world did you hang on for that long?" The truth I hear in them, and in myself even, is that it's never easy, and you have to find a way to hold on and hope with great faith. Those who don't hold on don't make it. The idea of jumping ship is always the most hopeless option. Don't folks know that if you jump ship, you'll drown?

I don't have any special formula on how to manage what hope looks like in your life, but you have to take action in order to achieve it. I recently went through the hardest time in my life. My husband and I have wanted to have a baby together since we got married. We prayed for it and fasted for it. Then, two years later, I was pregnant. Five weeks later, I lost it. And as if that wasn't hard enough, I was told that it is basically impossible to conceive on our own in the future. My hope was absolutely obliterated. I could not wrap my mind around what God could possibly have planned for that loss.

I was wrapped in this sorrowful blanket and couldn't see my way out. I could hardly bring myself to pray or read my Bible, and I hardly smiled. God's truths about me were miles away. I was mad at God and hurt by Him for allowing that to happen to me.

Then I had to work on bringing my mind back to reality. I got realigned with God so that I could hope again. I know God didn't do that to me. He allowed it, but He didn't do it. Then I took solace in knowing that He knows exactly what it feels like to lose a child in ways I'm thankful to never understand. That situation helped uncover many things that only loss could reveal, and things that are revealed can be worked on and healed. My recovery from the surgery, along with a mild case of COVID brought to my home, gave me a deeper ability to heal not only physically but also mentally and spiritually from what happened.

That time allowed me to find a newly energized hope in my Father. My God is a God of miracles, and what is meant for me will always be mine as long as I stay close to Him. I recalled that God is higher than any doctor or anything they can see. I know that if God wants us to bring another child into this world, He will do it, and it will be all Him. He will have every bit of Glory.

"Take a moment to remember who God is and who I am. There you go lifting my load again." ~Will Reagan and United Pursuit

These lyrics speak so much truth. When things aren't happening in the time frame or the way you'd like, if you're not careful, you may lose focus of who you are and who God really is. A setback could take place that throws you into a full-on identity crisis. You may think that your wait is finally over and that you're about to get everything you've been waiting for. Then it doesn't. Or you may see some great things happening to the people around you, yet nothing seems to be changing in your life. One small action or event can send you into a whirlwind of self-pity, discouragement, sadness, hurt, and so on. You start believing the negativity that's pouring in. Past pain may re-emerge. Then you begin to define what's going on based on circumstances from your past. This is what is called "making a mountain out of a molehill." Somehow, you lose sight of yourself, where you came from, what God brought you through, and who He says you are.

"For you created my inmost being; you knit me together in my mother's womb. I praise you because I am fearfully and wonderfully made; your works are wonderful, I know that full well." Psalms 139:13–14

God spent time on you. He knew exactly who you would be and what you would experience. He knew from day one that you could be trusted with this season of waiting. Jesus thought you were to die for. In those moments when you feel you will not receive your desires because you don't feel your worth, don't forget that you are a child of the King, and you are unconditionally loved, flaws and all.

Every now and then, you'll find that if you're in an insecure and hopeless place, you've probably traded your God-given truth for some lies about yourself and your situation. You end up believing you're worthless, insignificant, inadequate, or incapable and cannot do or have more than you do at that moment. If you've made it to that point, you've taken your eyes off of God. You're focusing on the waves instead of the hand holding you up, and you end up sinking—drowning in one foot of water when all you have to do is calm down, take your Father's hand, and stand up.

Our God is the biggest—meaning bigger than anything, ever, and forever. God is not just loving; He is love (1 John 4:6). He sees all. Knows all. He has His hand on ALL. He is the one who shields you from dangers you will never even know were there. He is the same God that never allows you to be crushed, no matter how crushed you think you are. I could go on all day, but I won't.

When you get back to the point of accepting the truth in the place where you are, especially when you're waiting, you can return to a place of peace. Holding to the truth will give you a surge of confidence that inevitably leads to contentment. You can be unburdened from feelings of lack and begin to walk lightly in your purpose even now. Take a moment to remember who God is and who you are, then watch how God lifts your load again.

CHAPTER 8

LET GO AND LET GOD

If we fail to really give our cares, worries, problems, dissatisfaction, and everything to Jesus, then trying to be patient in the waiting is a battle.

"Give your burdens to the LORD, and he will take care of you. He will not permit the godly to slip and fall." Psalms 55:22

God cares. There is a reason He allows us to call Him Father. As a mother, there are times when I know exactly what's going on or what's wrong with my teenage daughter. But I say nothing. I just want her to express her feelings in her own words. I want her to feel comfortable telling me what's going on with her and to know that she can trust me with what she's sharing. It doesn't matter if I already know. It doesn't even matter if I've already solved the problem without her knowing. She can tell me anyway because it's part of what strengthens our relationship.

God is clearly a way better parent than me. He is the ultimate parent. He feels the same way and much more about His children than I feel about mine. It doesn't matter if you've already asked God or told Him what you need a million times. He is ready and willing to hear what you have to say for a million and one more.

"Keep on asking, and you will receive what you ask for. Keep on seeking, and you will find. Keep on knocking, and the door will be opened to you. For everyone who asks, receives. Everyone who seeks, finds. And to everyone who knocks, the door will be opened." Matthew 7:7–8

Now, when I say give it to God, I don't mean going for the rocking chair method. You know, when you go to God, you tell Him what's up, but then you walk away still holding the issues you claimed you were giving to Him. Lean in to give it to God, then take it away over and over again like a rocking chair. There is no peace in that. No peace generally means no patience.

This concept is particularly hard for those of us who fall into the type-A category. We always need to know the plan. We also need a backup plan or three. We find it hard to trust when we can't be in the driver's seat. But if we treat God like this, doesn't that make Him no more than a sounding board? Is He not there for more than just hearing about your issues as you go on trying to solve them on your own? God can handle it, so trust Him and hand it over.

When you hand over your dreams, desires, and worries to God, try having a conversation with Him. I know it can be hard to hear from God, especially when we struggle to sit still and listen. But try. Maybe you'll hear the answers to your petitions a little better. He may give you some steps or instructions to follow. He may say you may need a few more tools or have a few more things to learn before your wait is up. He might tell you that you are ready, but what you're waiting for may not be. If you can't even let go and let God, as the saying goes, He can't tell you very much because you won't be in a place to receive anything else. You can't exactly receive anything new if your hands are full with the old. Is holding on worth it if it means missing out on something far better?

There is always a point when you have to let go. This doesn't mean that what you desire won't happen. You'll just be handing off those desires to God, and then you'll take a step back. Take a breather. Have a moment without being consumed by thoughts of whether or not anything is changing. We always hear that things happen when we least expect them. A long time ago, I worked in a restaurant, and one night they were doing some kind of raffle or contest or something. I was completely oblivious to this, so when I won this super-sized stuffed animal, I was completely in shock. Meanwhile, some of my coworkers were mad because they were putting real thought and effort into winning this prize. I was too busy doing my job that night to pay attention to a contest. Giving our situations to God can definitely happen this way. Give it up and get back to the work you are supposed to be doing now, and you never know what could happen. You may not get a humongous pink stuffed hedgehog as I did, but you will be delighted all the same.

If your desire is what is in God's will for you, and you are doing what is asked of you now, you don't have to hold on and try so hard. None of us has the power to make those kinds of changes anyway, but God does.

Stop worrying about the wrong things. Don't fall into the trap of being wrapped up in your own desires. All thoughts, actions, and prayers start bending toward those desires. Prayer life starts sounding repetitive. "God, bless me with what I'm asking for," "God, show me the steps to get to my desire," and so on. These prayers are okay, but is that all you're praying for? Life can't be so wrapped up in wants or even what we think we need.

"Seek first the kingdom of God and His righteousness, and all these things shall be added to you." Matthew 6:33

First of all, Jesus said this. Jesus didn't waste a breath, so pay attention. Getting consumed by desires leaves us seeking our wants first and maybe the kingdom later. We end up praying "gimmie gimmie" prayers. That would be okay if the kingdom came first. "Give me a pure heart" or "give me wisdom and discernment to navigate life the way God desires." You could say "gimmie" all day if that's what it looked like.

There was a beautiful time in my life when I could actually say that I was chasing God with my whole heart. Everything I did was to please my Father. Serving was a joy. I craved time in worship. I loved spending time with my fellow Christians. Somewhere along the line, this all became routine. I allowed it to lose its weight and become the "norm," and it was at this point of believing that I had the faith to walk down that my focus shifted. I knew that God was and would always be with me. I was going to church faithfully and was living the "right" way. I was a good Christian girl. So, it was okay in my mind to stop looking at Jesus and begin to increase my life from the world's viewpoint. You know, make more money, get a house, get a car, get a husband, have more kids, etc.; simply increase myself. I mean, at least God was in the vicinity. My logic was that I still prayed and read my Bible, so why not go for these things I've been waiting for? This thought process was a recipe for disaster. Not because what I wanted was wrong, but because I should've never taken my eyes off Jesus and completely pushed Him to the sidelines. He should never have become something I just do and not the whole reason for my being.

That temporary displacement of focus knocked me down. I was crushed, disappointed, lost, and lonely, and I became angry at God for a while. I had a job offer on the table, I was on track to purchase my first house, and there was a guy I believed had real potential in my life. One by one, and I mean back to back, it all fell apart. Not one of those things happened for me. All because I wanted everything, and I wanted it right then and had stepped out of God's covering to get it all. I was even madder at Him for telling me to start writing *this* book with *this* subject matter, just as I was being crushed by all of these letdowns.

But doesn't all of that display God's endless grace? I had pushed God aside to try to do things in my own power, yet He corrected me and still chose to pour into me. He gave me the wisdom and knowledge that were needed to pull me out of the difficult situation I had gotten myself into. He lovingly pulled me back into a place where He wanted me and even spared me from hard times that would've been far worse had He allowed any of what was presented to me to happen at that moment. If God had allowed me to keep pursuing what I wanted, I would've ended up living in an area far from my family, which would've made being a single mom harder. I would've ended up working in a horrible location known for its crime (definitely not a great thing when you work in banking). And my goodness, let's just say that things not working out with that guy was like taking the last flight out before the drop of an atom bomb. I thought at that moment my life was crashing all around me, but I just needed to hold on for a few more years for God to give me what He intended all along.

The things I wanted—things that many of us are programmed to want—are not actually bad. They can be good and even help serve kingdom purposes. The bad comes when these desires and wants are placed higher than God.

"So if you're serious about living this new resurrection life with Christ, act like it. Pursue the things over which Christ presides. Don't shuffle along, eyes to the ground, absorbed with the things right in front of you. Look up, and be alert to what is going on around Christ—that's where the action is. See things from his perspective." Colossians 3:1–2 MSG

Chase Jesus harder than you're chasing your desires. Chase Him like it's still fresh and new. Marvel at all He does for you, no matter how small, and I guarantee you that your patience will increase as you walk in and out of every season of life. Having all you want means nothing if Jesus has been brushed off in the search for it all. There is no point in gaining it all just to lose your soul and your first love. Our greatest anticipation should be to see Jesus face-to-face and to know and be known by Him. All else is indeed secondary.

"If you decide for God, living a life of God-worship, it follows that you don't fuss about what's on the table at mealtimes or whether the clothes in your closet are in fashion. There is far more to your life than the food you put in your stomach, more to your outer appearance than the clothes you hang on your body. Look at the birds, free and unfettered, not tied down to a job description, careless in the care of God. And you count far more to him than birds. Has anyone by fussing in front of the mirror ever gotten taller by so much as an inch? All this time and money wasted on fashion—do you think it makes that much difference? Instead of looking at the fashions, walk out into the fields and look at the wildflowers. They never primp or shop, but have you ever seen color and design quite like it? The ten best-dressed men and women in the country look shabby alongside them. If God gives such attention to the appearance of wildflowers—most of which are never even seen—don't you think he'll attend to you, take pride in you, do his best for you? What I'm trying to do here is to get you to relax, to not be so

preoccupied with getting, so you can respond to God's giving. People who don't know God and the way he works fuss over these things, but you know both God and how he works. Steep your life in God-reality, God-initiative, God-provisions. Don't worry about missing out. You'll find all your everyday human concerns will be met. Give your entire attention to what God is doing right now, and don't get worked up about what may or may not happen tomorrow. God will help you deal with whatever hard things come up when the time comes." Matthew 6:25–34

Human nature leads us to go a little or a lot crazy when we don't get what we want in a set timeframe. Adam and Eve started it. They were tempted to take a shortcut to knowledge. God walked with them in the garden, and they had full access to Him. That means that had they waited for God to return from wherever He went in the moment, they could've asked Him anything. God gave them EVERYTHING and only withheld evil and pain from them, rightfully so. Instead of waiting for God, they took matters into their own hands, and we're still paying for it. I sometimes ask God if it would be okay to slap them if they're in heaven when I get there.

But I can't really be that critical of them because we all do the same thing. We want to know everything now—the full and detailed plan and how it will be executed play-by-play. God is currently working things out for your good. Wait on Him. But again, that pesky human nature kicks in, which causes you to get anxious and worried. Then you end up biting your own apple.

By that, I mean you take matters into your own hands. "How can I make this happen? God and His plans are pushed aside. You may start hearing the whispers of worry. "If I can't see Him working, He must not be working." "Maybe He forgot about me or has some more important matters to attend to."

I was reminded of a great memory by way of social media this week. It was a reaction video of my daughter as she learned she was going on a cruise for her birthday. I planned and coordinated this trip with my family and chose to tell her nothing. I packed her bag in secret. We left late at night, so I put her in the car and told her to go back to sleep because we were going up the road. Even when she woke up in a completely different state, I still kept the surprise intact. I didn't reveal to her where we were actually going until we pulled up in front of the exact ship we were sailing on. The shrieks of pure excitement filled my heart with joy. But that is not the reason I chose to stay a mom.

Telling my then-6-year-old about her 7th birthday plans would have been good for no one. She would've started her kid-worrying. She would've asked me every day, multiple times a day, about when we were leaving. My kid is pretty Type A like her mom, so she would've started hovering over the packing process because, God forbid, I forget even one Hello Kitty or her favorite dress of the moment. Then she would go over the details of what she thought we should do on our trip. Keeping her oblivious saved her from all that unnecessary anxiety and saved me the headache of a million questions being thrown at me daily.

I'm her mother, and I love her. I knew everything that needed to happen and everything I needed to pack so that she had an amazing trip. And she did. As she's gotten older, I haven't had to coordinate any secret service missions, but I do have to keep her worry at bay. She still performs an extreme countdown, but she trusts me with the details because I haven't failed her yet.

Can we find our childlike faith that allows us to trust completely even though the waiting feels excruciating? If God can spend time making flowers look and smell so pretty, why wouldn't He spend even more time on you and what you're waiting for?

One day I was taking a walk through my neighborhood. I happened to look down at just the right moment and saw the tiniest little turtle on my path. This turtle was no bigger than the tip of my thumb. I then did something I never do. I picked it up. There were so many intricate details on this little guy. Numerous hues of green seemed to have been delicately hand-painted onto the shell and body. Details that would take serious effort and skill if anyone tried to recreate them, especially on such a small, delicate canvas. I was in awe over all this detail, all to help this little turtle hide among the grass. I was a bit mind-blown at the fact that all this attention was paid to something that pretty much never gets seen. God is definitely in the details.

Now back to you—uniquely created you, the only you that there will ever be. God built your frame with 206 different bones and covered them with muscles, tissues, and organs that make you function. He could've stopped there, and we could've just all looked like indistinguishable mannequins, but He chose to display His infinite artistry distinctively on each of us. In the history of time, no two identical humans have ever existed. Even twins have things that set them apart from each other. He determined whether you'd be born as a girl or a boy. He chose your complexion and the shapes of your eyes, nose, and ears. God formed exactly the smile He knew He'd be delighted to see every day you live, and He intentionally placed every hair on your head.

Our creative, careful, and loving God did all of this before you were even placed in your mother's belly. Do you think He would do all this and then leave you hanging? Do you really think He will overlook you while you obediently wait for Him? I highly doubt that. Why worry? The same God that breathed you into existence sees you and knows your every need and desire. He is delighted to take care of you.

What can worry do for you? It takes away from the very thing you are worrying about, yet it changes nothing. Worry won't make results happen any faster. If you just want to worry, I'll tell you what it can do. Worry creates stress, which is physically damaging to the body. It causes sickness and delays recovery. It's a great way to make your hair fall out and give yourself bad skin. Sleep will be horrible, as will your eating habits. The list goes on.

Mentally, worry prolongs things. Think about when you have to get some tests run at your doctor's office and then have to wait for the results. The wait for the results is one thing when it's just a routine checkup, but something entirely different if you feel something is a little off or wrong. If you're feeling good, you probably won't be thinking about the test results until they come. Weeks could go by, and you wouldn't have given them a second thought. Meanwhile, if you're waiting on test results for something potentially life-changing, those results will be on your mind constantly. You will frequently check your phone for missed calls or your inbox in case the doctor chooses to send an email. You may even begin calling your doctor every day just to check. As much as you wish it would, all of this worry and fuss won't change the length of time it takes to process those tests and send you the results. But that same worry could make two days feel like two years.

I once heard a saying: "You can't stop the birds from flying by, but you can stop them from building a nest." This is some of the best knowledge I've received in my life. The mind is truly a battlefield, and the fights of the mind go on the longest and have a deeper effect than any outside affliction. Mind wars tend to happen as we allow what should be a passing thought to come in and take root, then grow into something wild that is hard to dig up. Worry sprouts roots very quickly.

Long periods of waiting can really do a number on the mind, and it can be like one of those wrestling brawls where all the wrestlers come out of nowhere to attack as you try to keep those negative thoughts from taking over. You might be walking, and something would remind you of what you want. Like walking through the mall right after you decide to get back in control of your health and fitness, and you smell freshly baked cones coming from the ice cream shop, just like a cartoon character that catches a whiff of something wonderful, and the smell has them floating away. In a perfect world, that reminder would make you stop, maybe say a prayer about that desire, thank God for the work He's doing behind the scenes, and then go on enjoying your day. Unfortunately, it doesn't always go like that. Sometimes you'll let that distracting thought take you away if you don't keep your guard up.

Maybe you'll think about what it will be like to have what you're waiting for. Not so bad. But then that thought trickles into a stream. You begin to wonder if it'll ever happen at all for you. Then that stream of thoughts turns into a river of wondering about all your inadequacies and insecurities, as well as all the reasons you think you're being held back. If unchecked, this river will become an ocean of Ds—doubt, discouragement, and disappointment. Now you're drowning all because you saw a picture, heard a song, read a headline, or whatever the trigger was. Maybe just smelling an ice cream cone makes you believe you look horrible when you actually could've acknowledged the smell and kept going about your day just as contently as you had been just a moment prior.

A few years back, at a church small group night, someone made a great point. Anytime the devil wanted to get into someone's head, he did so by inserting doubt by way of questioning or throwing in "if" scenarios. He questioned Eve in the garden. He questioned God in regard to Job's faithfulness. He had the audacity to question Jesus multiple times in the desert during His time of fasting. So, of course, he is going to keep playing that same old, used-up card on us. The devil is really not all that creative in his attempts to get us into our own heads and make us doubt. He tries to make us doubt what God said to us, who God says we are, and who we believe we are.

Let's go on and call this another enemy tactic. The devil knows that if he can whisper enough lies in your ears, your mental state will begin to crack. If he can get to your mind, then he can affect your heart, which will, in turn, dampen your spirit. Satan will try to plant a seed in our minds to get in his question, which will lead us to question ourselves and God. He may start with, "Did God really say that to you?" Then your mind may take it a step further with, "What if that's not what God meant?" "What if that wasn't God at all?" "What if this never happens for me?" and so on.

I don't even want to think about the things I've missed out on because one stupid question made me doubt myself so much that I was paralyzed. I've skipped out on events because the questioning made me feel insecure enough to doubt if anyone would care whether I was there or not. There are friendships that I didn't pursue because I was led to doubt if they would be able to handle my odd personality type. There have been points in writing this book where I have stopped because I questioned whether or not God really wanted ME to write it, which made me doubt if anybody would want to read anything I would write. After all, who am I anyway? Then I questioned if writing this was going to have any real purpose. I had to get one of those TV slaps to snap me out of it so I could remember that God said to just do it and not worry about the rest.

It's an all-out war sometimes, trying to get back to the position of hope and faith you were in before that horrible whisper in your ear. Those questions end up throwing a wild and uncontrollable party that seems impossible to tame. Now you can't even embrace the promise God has given you or enjoy what He sends your way because doubt and confusion have taken over. That doubt starts pulling you away from what you need to do. That's where we come back to see our prayer life begin to fade. The joy soon follows, and then we just end up in a place where all we can see is lack and what isn't happening. Push back at the lies. Take authority over what you allow to dwell in your mind. Fight back.

"We demolish arguments and every pretension that sets itself up against the knowledge of God, and we take captive every thought to make it obedient to Christ." 2 Corinthians 10:5

This scripture has saved me from and pulled me out of those crazy questioning rabbit holes plenty of times. I h ad to make it personal. Whenever a negative thought or a lie about myself would creep in, I would recite, "I take this lie and I submit it to Jesus." I would repeat it over and over again, and sometimes I would even say it out loud to chase those thoughts away. I may have scared a few strangers over the years, but it worked. Some days take more effort than others, but it's always worth it for the truth to stand its ground in your mind. You have to take hold of what God said to you and chase all the nonsense out immediately. Find scriptures that you can use in your battle. Write them down. You may have to do something I've done in the past: write them on sticky notes and put them on your mirror or door so you can see them and speak life into your season of waiting.

God knows you're waiting. The wait is not a punishment. Calm down, relax, and let God do what He's going to do. *"What I'm trying to do here is to get you to relax, to not be so preoccupied with getting, so you can respond to God's giving"* *(Matthew 6:31)*. Don't worry so much about what you're getting or not getting; rather, focus on what God is giving you now and what He has already given. Count your blessings and endure, because He can and will come through again and again for you. No need to worry.

CHAPTER 9

GOD SAID REST

It's quite easy to get sucked into the busyness of trying to obtain your goals and desires. We often forget to rest in the now. That rest could help us to recharge completely so we can be energized, awake, and able to handle what the next stage of life brings when the wait is finally over. It also allows us to sit back and get a fresh view of what's going on. It's easier to see the big picture when you pause.

I've had times when I was running on fumes. The gas light in me had been on for miles, yet I was continuously pushing it. Nothing is clear in that state. Thoughts just run all over each other. Rationality starts to fade away. Waiting feels like the end of the world. The exhaustion will make everything seem far worse than it is. If the wind blows the wrong way, everything could come crashing down. Crazy how something as simple as getting a full night's sleep and taking a day to mentally, physically, and spiritually recharge can solve everything—or at least put you in a better position to handle it all.

In 2017, I was house hunting. At that moment, I thought I was ready. I had been approved for a loan, and a budget was set. I had all I needed for a deposit and a little extra in savings. I was excited. Somehow, the house hunt became a mad dash. I was constantly on listing sites, and I saw house after house after house. I had tunnel vision for a moment and was quickly worn out from this crazy process. I was so busy with the search that I failed to pause and look at all the warning signs. Nothing was stacking up. I initially had an unlicensed real estate agent, which I found out about a few weeks in. My hours at work were dwindling because I was a floater going into the slow season, yet my expenses were increasing. The houses in my budget were either way too far away or just plain horrible. When I finally found a place to bid on, the HOA was so high that my daughter and I had to light the place with candles, use our neighbors' showers, and house-hop for our daily meals because I most definitely would have been underwater trying to pay for it all.

So, I finally chose (although it felt more like being forced) to step back. In doing so, I could see the situation more clearly. I was not in a dire situation where I just had to move. I simply felt desperate for change. The reality was that I had a roof over my head and a unique ability to save money. I could see that moving to some of the areas I was looking at would've made it difficult for me to receive help with my daughter. Most of all, I could see that I did NOT want to cut grass or do any maintenance.

I'm beyond grateful for that pause. I didn't want to wait anymore at the moment, but the waiting led to some better blessings for me. God chose to move me from one waiting room to another. Starting in February 2018, I kept hearing God say, "You don't know where you'll be in a year." Yay! More waiting. I didn't look at it that way. But I knew that whatever move I made at that point would be temporary because God had something stewing for me. God blessed me so much once I took that step back. He blessed me with a new position, which came with a pay increase and stability. I moved into an apartment, and God took my idea of what I thought I could afford and doubled it. I was in the exact location I always dreamed I'd move to, and my daughter was able to start middle school in a fantastic school district. A year later, my husband was on the scene, and I wasn't bound to any situation. We got married right when my lease was up. Prayer after prayer answered and increased all as a result of rest.

Thanks to that rest, I was able to look back and see that what I wanted at the moment was certainly not what I needed. But as always, God knew better. We can never truly see what lies ahead of us in any season, no matter how much we plan and prep, so it's good to sit back, relax, and let God do the heavy lifting.

"It is useless for you to work so hard from early morning until late at night, anxiously working for food to eat; for God gives rest to His loved ones." Psalms 127:2

You'll end up burned out when you're on a nonstop pursuit. Sit back and rest. When you know you have a long day ahead filled with work, meetings, afterschool activities, cooking, etc., it's far easier to handle it if you've gotten a full 8 hours of sleep and a cup of coffee in the morning. I know I'm still fairly young, happily in my thirties, but I've had more than enough experience to know that seasons of waiting and stagnancy tend to be followed by a lot of action. In just one moment, things can go from the mundane "same old, same" to a full-speed sprint. You never know what's ahead of you, so rest. Rest every part of yourself so that you will be energized for what's to come.

Rest allows for a change of focus or perspective, for sure. Constantly being on the go, even when you're doing good, will cause you to miss everything. It's hard to enjoy the moment and fully grasp what God is doing when you're too busy to see it. Think about the story of Mary and Martha when Jesus came to their house with the disciples. Martha was busy with the details. She was prepping the house, making food for her guests, and all around being a good hostess. She wasn't doing anything wrong, but she was missing it. Mary understood the moment. She had Jesus in her house. She chose to rest at His feet and take in everything He had to say.

I do a lot of hosting in my home, so I can definitely relate to Martha. I've had many occasions where I put so much into planning a party or event that I didn't get a chance to enjoy those events. I very much realized this after Amai's 5th birthday. I spent about two months and a good bit of money on that party. I totally missed it. Everyone else had a great time, but I was exhausted and wasn't able to enjoy any of it. I then understood why people hired help for these things.

In my young 20s, I had a lot going on. Many times, I would just go until I dropped. I was like the people who see the gas light come on in the car and get adventurous. Rather than stop at the gas station, they rationalize that they can go about 10 more miles before the engine cuts off. If that is you, stop it. I was not like that in my car, but I was like that in life. I had a little high-energy child living the single-mom life. At points, I had two jobs, was in school, served at church, and tried to show up to all the social events. I would go at that so hard that I would have panic attacks. I'd be at an event and just want to ball up in a corner and cry. It didn't help that I was trying to push past the fact that I am a secret introvert.

I would do this to myself over and over. I'd even question the idea of rest every time I heard it preached. I figured that the Sabbath was not created for the single mother. There was no way. The anxiety and the burnout would always come out in the wrong way, as they always tend to do. My patience for my daughter was next to none. I yelled a lot more than I'd like to admit. I had to figure it out. When she was younger, I had to first figure out Sabbath moments, which, for many of us, are when we pull up in front of the grocery store or the house and take about 30 minutes before going in just for a moment of solitude. I still do this often.

Sometimes I would force that alone time in quite late at night after bedtime because that was all I had. Later on, I was able to incorporate "rest" into my morning walks. I carved out as little or as much time as I could, walking alone and talking to Jesus.

As she got older and it got easier to get my parents to babysit, I'd rest by having girls' nights out where I could talk through whatever was going on in life while taking off all the responsibility hats. I've now made it a point to take child-free vacations where I can get away and reset. As a single mom, that meant planning and setting strict savings goals while also doing whatever was needed.

All of these little and great things help me to rest, recharge, and refocus. I am a better mom, a better friend, a better employee, a better wife—just all around better with rest. I lay out those examples in the hopes that if you struggle with finding ways to rest, you can start figuring out what rest looks like for you.

For some people, lying around and doing nothing is restful. If that's you, go for it. We all should sit around and be vegetables now and then. Your rest could come through in some sort of activity. In the last year or so, I've realized that painting and crafting are great ways for me to decompress and refocus. My husband definitely gets calm when he takes care of all his turtles and fish in his office aquarium. It can be whatever it needs to be, as long as you rest.

Make the most of your vacation time. The job will be there when you get back. Many people care for their job far more than the job takes care of them. If it is offered to you, take it without guilt. It's yours. And if you are that person who struggles with taking their allotted time, turn your phone off when you do go, so you're not tempted to give away your time. Take a pause. Like really. Don't take a day off and do housework and run errands; really take some time off. If you can, go somewhere and relax. If you can't go somewhere, then have a staycation. I know it can be hard, but dedicate time to nothing. Don't cook, clean, fold clothes, do yard work, grocery shop, or do anything that is considered work. If you can take more than one day, do all of those things on your first day, then relax.

Sleep in. Order some food or go out to eat. Spend some time with God. Read a book or catch up on your favorite shows. Maybe go to the gun range or a painting class. I personally love taking trips to the beach during the off-season with no kids, so I can look and listen to the ocean. Do whatever will calm your mind, body, and spirit.

We should all do better with self-care and our mental health. In the US, we are taught to just "go, go, go," and everything has to happen right now. I love going to the Caribbean and experiencing Island Time. Go to a restaurant, and your food comes when it comes. You're forced to kill the rush, enjoy the scenery, and be patient. And man, if the food isn't always worth the wait. You may have even made a friend. Show up when you get there and leave when you're done. Every time I go down, I see and meet people over 90, and sometimes over 100, who look carefree and rested. Why? Because they know how to relax and not stress over everything.

Rested people perform better. Thinking is so much clearer when the clutter has had time to be cleared out. Rest makes room for you to be able to be joyful and for you to handle life better all around. If God, being God, said that He needed a day, do we think we are more capable than God? We most certainly are not. Running through rest will just leave you exhausted, and exhaustion leads to burnout. The Bible says, "Do not get burned out on doing good." Shoot, don't get burned out at all. Take your time to rest so you can live life to its fullest potential. Rest so that when your waiting period is over, you will be much more ready to execute all that God has for you.

CHAPTER 10

NO OTHER OPTION

Stop acting like you have another option. Sure, you have endless options by "normal standards," but not really. Once God has placed a plan in you, anything else passing for a possibility is just a counterfeit.

Counterfeit: made in exact imitation of something valuable or important with the intention to deceive or defraud.

Counterfeits do their best to look like the real thing. Some are obvious, like someone trying to sell you a Lewis Vitton purse or an Inviction watch. They may look good at first glance, but those little typos let you know the lie. Some forgeries require a closer look. Something may be slightly less shiny. Or, much like counterfeit money, you may have to shine a light on it to check for authenticity.

"Dear friends, do not believe everyone who claims to speak by the Spirit. You must test them to see if the Spirit they have

comes from God. For there are many counterfeits in the world."
1 John 4:1

Be careful, because counterfeits can unleash a full-fledged attack on you and possibly those around you as well. These fakes are meant to blend in with normal currency. The thing is, if you don't catch the fake at the beginning, you'll be left with less than what you began with. Not only will you lose the value of what the counterfeit was pretending to be, but you'll also walk away without whatever you were trying to gain.

Say you run into one of these imitations in a relationship (friendship, dating, coworker, or anyone you deal with). Once you find out about the fraud, you will not just lose that person; you probably gave up time, energy, money, hopes, emotions, and so on to build something with them. Sadly, phonies are everywhere. The devil himself tries to place things in front of us disguised as lovely when, in reality, they're all poison.

"I am not surprised! Even Satan disguises himself as an angel of light. So it is no wonder that his servants also disguise themselves as servants of righteousness." 2 Corinthians 11:14–15

Don't let this daunt you. God will give you a heads-up. He can train you to see past any cunning façade. But you have to pay attention. Examine what's being presented to you. Hold it up against the light and see what's missing.

My single years were filled with counterfeit meetings. I waited a long time in purity and patience (most of that time).

Many "options" presented themselves over the years. These "options" were often visually appealing and looked great on paper. God gave me a vision for my marriage many years in advance, so I had to be careful not to try to make a replica fit into my original picture. What's the alternative? Yeah, I could've dated the next cute guy who had a job and all of his teeth. I might have even fallen for him if I wanted to. I could have very well ended up married to that guy. But accepting said random guy would've been the result of me trying to end my wait and get what I thought I wanted at the moment. I would've been settling for less than what God wanted for me. I also knew that if I moved out of God's will, I set myself up for pain and disappointment on so many different levels. So having "options" was no option at all for me. The options are to either wait or wait. I knew then, and I know now that God won't fail me.

If God has laid out a specific career path for you, hold on to that plan. Having something in the meantime is probably just fine, but don't take a position that will deter you and keep you away from chasing the desire to do what God wants you to do and what deep down you want to be doing. You may end up stuck settling for just a regular old job that you will eventually burn out on because it's all money and no joy.

Why settle for less than God's best? What if, in settling for the right now option, you miss out on what was set apart for you? What if you go ahead and settle for Mr. Right Now, and the man who could actually be Mr. Right appears but has to keep on walking because you are taken? What if your dream house is listed on the market at a price far below what it's worth, but you've just locked yourself into a 12-month lease and have no ability to buy your way out? No, it's not the end of the world, and God is all about second chances. He can send around another opportunity, but you will be waiting that much longer. Why entertain these counterfeits and accept them as options? Your only option should be to walk in God's will, no matter the circumstances.

No matter how long it takes, allow God to take away your options and backup plans. Oh, and also let Him have the backup plan to the backup plan. A lot of us were taught to have a contingency plan in case things don't work out, you change your mind, or it all blows up in your face. Basically, don't trust anything entirely unless you're able to control it yourself.

College students are often encouraged to have a major and a minor. If he can't be a doctor, at least he can be a teacher. A person on a job hunt puts out multiple applications at various businesses because if the desired option doesn't call back, one of the others will. It's fine to be ready for any outcome, but with God, setting up these options is not necessary at all.

"Trust in the Lord with all your heart; do not depend on your own understanding. Seek His will in all you do, and He will show you which path to take." Proverbs 3:5-6

The Lord knows how His children struggle with this application. I am the type of person who resists letting anyone drive me anywhere. They may not drive at the speed I like or brake as smoothly as I think they should. Some people I know drive so crazy that I have to hold on and pray the entire ride. Essentially, they don't drive like me. I am actively working on this, and my husband can attest to my efforts. Aside from him, I opt to put my life in my own hands and rarely trust anyone to get me where I need to go safely. God often gets this "other driver" treatment from us. We eagerly get into the passenger seat, and as the song goes, let Jesus take the wheel. It starts off smooth and lovely as you start down the road. But then God takes an unexpected turn. Um ok. That is not the way you wanted to go. Next, you notice that He is driving really slowly, like actually staying within the speed limit. You then start plotting and trying to figure out how you can get God to pull over so you can have an Uber take you the rest of the way because you will never get there if this keeps going on. But now He's taking you up some mountain with all these snakes turns. You know, the kind where if the wind blows too hard, you'll be flying right over the edge. At some point, you end up holding on to that handle that is meant to hang clothes on as though it could do anything at all to save you. That's about how I feel when God is guiding me through the waiting. God, could we not have taken the easier, smoother route?

Sometimes God gets pushed out of the driver's seat when we think we can do better, only to find that we have no clue where we're going or how to get there. After wasting the time it took to figure that out; hopefully, we will have enough sense to return the keys to God, get back in the passenger seat, and wait patiently as He guides us on our way.

Letting God drive means we don't have to plan alternative routes. You don't need backup destinations, just in case. He doesn't have the ability to fail. He takes all the plans and preparations we make and exchanges them for better, more perfect plans designed uniquely for each of us. No replica is possible.

"By coming up with a new plan, a new covenant between God and his people, God put the old plan on the shelf. And there it stays, gathering dust." Hebrews 8:13

Another version of that scripture ends by saying, *"It is now out of date and will soon disappear."* If you're struggling to stay patient and get the urge to set up a plan B or even think of accepting a knock-off option, take this scripture and make it personal. All these other things are a waste of time and will end up disappearing in the wind soon enough. A better plan is already happening. Wait for it.

Is it really trusting God when we keep setting up all of these safety nets? Aren't these nets evidence that we believe we may fall and God doesn't have the ability to save us? I pray that we all know that even if we do fall, God can and will catch us and place us back on firm ground. In reality, we often end up trapped in those nets. This happens when we make the backup plan the main plan, probably as a result of believing that God is dragging His feet. Just because we can't see what's going on behind a momentarily closed door, we start working on trying to open another. Just chill.

God may be sending you on a life-changing mission to another country. Don't call yourself starting something else because you can't see how the finances will come together. God may have freed up space in your life to start using your talents to build something great. Try to fight the desire to go do something safe that will keep you from doing it. Avoid moving in with someone who will have a negative impact on your life (no matter the relationship type) only because you want to pay less rent. Those are the fakes masquerading as the plan.

How can God come through if you won't move out of the way and let Him do so? God is such a gentleman, and He will never force His ways and plans on you. The exchange is up to you. Give God your options and even your non-options that you'd only consider when you get extremely impatient, anxious, bored, lonely, or whatever. If God sees fit to remove the failsafe, the unnecessary debris, and all the fakes, let Him do it. He is making room in your life and in your heart for something new and much better. Let all the fear of falling be pushed to the side and wait confidently as God unfolds a victory for you.

Which do you prefer?

Which is greater to you—God or the gift? In the Bible, we've seen waiting turn into idolatry so many times. Moses was only gone for about a month and a half (forty days), and the Israelites lost it. The people exchanged the real thing (God) for some horrible counterfeits in the form of golden cows. I will never understand that logic.

"When the people saw how long it was taking Moses to come back down the mountain, they gathered around Aaron. 'Come on,' they said, 'make us some gods who can lead us. We don't know what happened to this fellow Moses, who brought us here from the land of Egypt.'" Exodus 32:1

Rather than waiting forty days to allow God to continue to lead them into the promised land, they allowed themselves to be led by the gifts they possessed (gold, silver, and wood). God, the one that literally parted the sea to free them, was pushed aside for things that had very little present value and absolutely no eternal value. They turned to idols that left them wandering until they died, and they were never able to take hold of what God wanted to give them.

Maybe idolatry isn't so literal with us, but we are still guilty of doing the same. When we think God is taking too long, we end up giving our desires prime real estate in our hearts and minds, pushing God off into a corner for us to pick up when we feel like it. We stop waiting for God and begin following or even chasing what we want instead. Sorry to say, but that is idolatry.

To my single and waiting friends, have you ever become a little consumed by the thought of your future spouse? I've been guilty of this. I've had times when I only talked to God to ask for my husband. In times when I met someone, I would do my best to try to force fit them into what God wanted for me. Then I would end up wrapped in some dude who could never fit into the place God carved out specifically for my future husband. But no, I'd give all my time and energy to some guy that was only pulling me further and further away from my time with God.

After God is put out of view for that thing, whatever it is, we make it worse by only pulling God out of the corner to be treated like a genie or just to talk about the very thing you've now placed above Him. That's like if your sweetie just left you for someone else, married them, and then called you to see if that was cool with you. That's horrible. Or maybe you hit God with the "gimmie," "let me get a...," or "please, please" types of prayers. Even though you've come with a prayer, the desire still means more than really spending that time with God. It's no wonder God sometimes has to push the pause button on our desires. Sometimes we have to be given a thorn to bring our focus back.

"Because of the extravagance of those revelations, and so I wouldn't get a big head, I was given the gift of a handicap to keep me in constant touch with my limitations. Satan's angel did his best to get me down, what he in fact did was push me to my knees. No danger then of walking around high and mighty. At first, I didn't think of it as a gift, and begged God to remove it. Three times I did that and then He told me, "My grace is enough, it's all you need. My strength comes into its own in your weakness." Once I heard that, I was glad to let it happen. I quit focusing on the handicap and began appreciating the gift. It was a case of Christ's strength moving in on my weakness. Now I take limitations in stride, and with good cheer, those limitations that cut me down to size—abuse, accidents, opposition, bad

breaks. I just let Christ take over. And so the weaker I get, the stronger I become." 2 Corinthians 12:7–10

Have you been viewing your wait as a limitation? I definitely have. Maybe if we looked at the gift rather than the handicap, we could experience true joy and contentment while we wait. Setbacks, delays, and stumbles will try to knock us off track. Satan will do the most as he attempts to take us out. Let him try. Go on and let all these things push you to your knees. Let the difficulties allow you to spend more time at the feet of Jesus. They will bring out your weaknesses and make way for God's power in your life.

Let God do what He wants to do, even if it feels like a handicap. Accept your thorns because, much like the thorns on the stem of a rose, they are just the base of something beautiful. They may be protecting you from harm that could halt or inhibit your flower from blooming; concede to that protection. That protection could even be from yourself.

"God, take this wait away!" It feels like such a burden, and definitely more so after a good amount of time has passed. Each day that passes requires much more work to hold on to faith and hope. For the most part, I have been able to see that God is trusting me with my wait. Much like a thorn in my side, there are days when waiting is utterly painful, while at other times, that thorn seems to blend right in with my everyday life, and I hardly notice it at all. Naturally, when the pain seems to be at its greatest, those are the moments that I am pushed to pray more. That's when I'm really having to count the cost of what it means to keep enduring and what I lose if I let go at this point. In those moments, I get to make the choice all over again to wait on God because His way always beats anything else. I can be the little girl who takes her broken pieces to Daddy and lets Him fix me up again.

When did God stop being enough? When did life turn from pursuing God's presence to pursuing the gifts He can give? Desires must be kept in their proper place. The realization of these desires can't be the end-all and be-all of your life. They can't determine whether or not you will experience joy. All great things come from God but are completely useless without Him.

"So don't be misled, my dear brothers and sisters. Whatever is good and perfect is a gift coming down to us from God our Father, who created all the lights in the heavens." James 1:16–17

Why is having a life full of God, even as you wait, not sufficient? Let's do a heart check. Think about the thing you desire most right now. Picture it clearly, and imagine yourself with it. Then imagine that it never happens or that you never get it. Ever. Now be completely honest with yourself as I pose the next question. Remember, God already knows your heart, so there is no good Sunday school answer. Would living a life waiting for something that will never happen strain or even end your relationship with God? Or if you received your desire only to have it taken away at some point, would you walk away from your life with Jesus? If so, you may have an idol on your hands. You may even need to put that desire down for a time and put God back into the leading place in your life.

A couple of years ago, I crashed into great disappointment. I mentioned before about all of my biggest desires seeming to be so close and attainable, but then every single one of those things was pulled away from me. Two job positions with great pay, I just knew they would easily be mine. Homeownership. Just the right set of friends. Church life was thriving. The guy. All within a short timeframe snatched away from me.

I'll be transparent here. I turned every one of those things into an idol. I figured I had a handle on all of these things, so God was unintentionally removed from the process of making things happen in my life. I gave all of my time to focus on getting these things. I spent my free time house hunting. My mind was completely wrapped up in this guy. I wasn't praying any real prayers; I was just talking at God. My worship time was limited only to Sundays when I could bother to be on time for church. My time in scripture was limited to pressing play on the Bible app as I dozed off to sleep, hardly hearing a word. It was definitely a moment where the gifts had way more weight than the Giver.

Thankfully, I was convicted (I did not feel thankful at the moment at all). One by one, all those things I thought I was about to have just fell away. Exhaustion ended the house hunt. Ran away from the church God placed me in, only to be sent right back. The guy was taken away, which was great because it turned out I was chasing way more than any woman of value should (that's all women). And both jobs went away, which was great because the commute to either would've caused great strain on my life.

Idols are pointless for anything other than instant, yet fleeting, gratification. Every one of those things I was trying so hard to attach myself to at the moment seemed just amazing and would have done me so much harm. The Israelites were left roaming in the desert for forty years because of their idols. Had I continued to follow mine, I would've still been roaming aimlessly away from God's plan for my life.

"Troubles multiply for those who chase after other gods." *Psalms 16:4*

It's a wise action to examine the placement of our desires. Many were put in our hearts by God and are very good, but they do not define us. We will not die without them. They do not determine whether or not our lives will be filled with purpose and peace. Desires are meant to add, not take over. When choosing between which is more important, having your desire from now until you die or having God from now until eternity, even when it hurts, choose God. He is the one with the power to fulfill all your needs and wants.

CHAPTER 11

PURPOSED FOR MORE

If you can relate to the way David came across from time to time in the Psalms, you may wonder here and there if God has forgotten you. I know I can definitely feel that. *"My God, my God, why have you abandoned me? Why are you so far away when I groan for help?" (Psalms 22:1).*

That feeling is definitely a result of the impatience of the flesh. God said, *"I will never fail you. I will never abandon you" (Hebrews 13:5).* We need to choose daily to accept this, as tough as life's circumstances tend to get. We also have to accept that we are special and that God has a special purpose for each of us. He will not take you and use you for every single thing. You will be worn out quickly that way.

"In a wealthy home, some utensils are made of gold and silver, and some are made of wood and clay. The expensive utensils are used for special occasions, and the cheap ones are for everyday use. If you keep yourself pure, you will be a special

utensil for honorable use. Your life will be clean, and you will be ready for the master to use you for every good work." 2 Timothy 2:20-21

You are not a spork. Feel free to be a little confused and even slightly amused by this profound revelation, because I was definitely both when God said this to me. When God told me this, I burst out laughing right in the middle of work and could not stop laughing about it until the next day. He certainly does have a great sense of humor. Let me explain. A spork tries to be multipurpose, but it really isn't all that great at anything other than making lines in your mashed potatoes—the lines you start drawing out of boredom because you're pretty much done trying to eat that fast-food delight. You absolutely do not want to try to eat a steak with one of these, as I'm sure it would break on impact. Eating soup with a spork will keep you there all day in frustration because it can't hold liquid very well. In case you aren't familiar with a spork, you will generally find them at your fast-food chicken joints. If you couldn't tell by the name, it is a sad union between a spoon and a fork. The only thing you can successfully eat with one is mashed potatoes, and even that could be done better with a spoon.

Again, God has purposed you for more. Like a golden knife used only by high society for the most exquisite dishes or a crystal tray that is carried with extreme caution to display a beautiful feast. These items are stored in a special place, not among the plastic or paper plates. They are cleaned with specific products, not those you grab on the fly because they are on sale.

They will be placed in beautiful oak curios or cabinets lined with special materials for long-term storage.

What I want to focus on here is the fact that these special utensils are generally stored for long periods of time before they are used. They are pulled out only for holidays, weddings, or other significant events. When the cabinet is finally opened, everyone knows something great is about to happen. Then, when the utensils are pulled out, you will find no scratches or stains, and if your mom were as serious about her china cabinet as mine was, you wouldn't even find a single fingerprint.

You might be able to relate more to caring for watches, jewelry, shoes, cars, or whatever is your treasure. If we are this careful with earthly treasures, why do we expect God to treat the treasures in us any less? He knows the exact moment to let those treasures out. He won't waste your value on everyday use.

Someone reading this may have the gift of preaching. God is not going to instruct you to preach 24/7 and everywhere you go. You won't be preaching to the dog, to the same neighbor every day, to random people passing by, to your coworkers all the time, or even to the preacher. People will think you're crazy, and you'll be worn out quickly, especially since about 99% of the people may not listen, no matter how amazing and truthful your preaching is. There is a time and place for everything, as it says in Ecclesiastes.

Instead, God will grow and cultivate that gift in you and release it at a time when you have the audience to whom He wants you to deliver it. He'll make sure that sharing your gift will give you and those who hear your life. If you preach to every single ear you come across, by the time you make it to your intended platform, you will be exhausted and worn out by the rejection of speaking to so many deaf ears. Your delivery won't be as pure, joyful, energetic, or hopeful as it would've been had you waited for God to tell you when to go.

I've jumped the gun on using my gifts in the past. I know God has given me the great gift of being able to bring people together, as well as the gift of encouragement. I knew that God had placed a desire in my heart to lead groups of women. I had done it successfully in the past in the form of a small group through the church I was attending at the time. It was a great and fulfilling season until God moved me on to the next thing. I later received multiple requests from a couple of ladies to put together a new group. After enough of their nudging, I decided (without God) to try to form this new small group. While I indeed possessed the tools and giftings, God did not say that it was time to do this sort of thing. So, the group never took off, and I was left feeling disappointed and discouraged by the process. Had I chosen to include God in my decision and waited for His green light, I would have had a completely different outcome. I was treating my special utensil like a spork. Thankfully, God wiped away the little smudge I made and put me back in the position I needed to be in until the special occasion meant for me arrived.

I had no clue that it would take over five years for God to give me a clear vision of what group of women I should be leading. I had a lot more to experience to build me up to the point of leadership God wanted me in. He has since given me a heart for moms from all walks of life. I had to experience motherhood from multiple angles to gain the wisdom and authority needed to lead moms into a community. I had to wait so that I could experience life as a single mom. A mom without honor roll kids. A married mom. A working mom. A blended family mom. A mom that has lost. A mom who has hustled. And so much more. God gave me the vision to lead early on so I would be prepared when the time came. It wasn't for me to dive ten toes in right away. God has always understood each special gift He has given me, and He is always right on time with the release.

"This vision is for a future time... If it seems slow in coming, wait patiently, for it will surely take place. It will not be delayed." Habakkuk 2:3

Alright, if the spork thing threw you off, I get it. The idea is much like the story of Esther. She was clearly not just some random chick. She was hand-picked to be among many virgins to be considered for the king to take as his wife. That alone would've been a huge honor. The request for a virgin already made it clear that she had to be set apart and not used up and thrown away like a spork. You can't make a spork a queen! That would be ridiculous. Forgive me for going back to the spork. I'll move on. For a year, Esther received beauty and skin treatments so she would be presentable as a queen. I'm sure she also had to be taught what it would be like to live as a queen and what rules would be followed when dealing with her future husband, the king.

Only after all of that preparation and waiting could she be presented to the king. Esther was given a special purpose by God. Clearly, she was beautiful and very likely kind and intelligent as well. But she didn't waste it. She didn't give her time and energy to the men who, I'm sure, approached her. She didn't give in to temporary pleasures and distractions that would've taken her out of the running. Because she allowed herself to be set aside for a special time and a special purpose, she was given the favor to approach her king and carry out her purpose, which was to save her people.

"Who knows if perhaps you were made queen for just such a time as this?" Esther 4:14

God knows. Thankfully, Jesus came, so we can be presented as pure, beautiful, and full of favor in the same way that Esther was. It is up to us to allow ourselves to be saved for "such a time as this." We are in control of whether we are to be used and tossed like a spork or if we want to be saved for those rare occasions like a 24k cutlery set meant for use at royal occasions.

Being in the china cabinet for a long time can be tough. It sometimes stinks to be the golden tableware as you watch the plastic ware being used all the time. Ugh, there goes the plastic coming out for the chicken nuggets and mac and cheese. Here we go again for spaghetti night. Seriously, is no one getting married this week? Not even a retirement party? The special stuff may not be used every day, but the level of care taken to prepare you is amazing. Just like Esther, special utensils are prepared before use. They will be taken out to be cleaned and polished. All scratches and blemishes will be removed. The utensils will be pristine and laid out beautifully in a special arrangement when it's finally time for them to be used.

Your master knows why He purchased you. He knows that you are beautiful—a one-of-a-kind creation made with a unique purpose. He won't leave you there to be forgotten. You don't want to be the plasticware or even the everyday utensils, because those are thrown out and replaced frequently. Meanwhile, even though you may only be used on rare occasions, you will be kept forever, and your value increases as time goes on.

This is how it goes as God releases us from waiting. The feeling of being shelved can leave you feeling forgotten. But really, God is just preparing the way for you and setting up all the details worthy of your special talents.

"I knew you before I formed you in your mother's womb. Before you were born, I set you apart..." Jeremiah 1:5

God has a plan for each of us. Desires are placed uniquely in us. We have to let those desires trump the ones we've created on our own. Emotions have to be set aside so we can confidently wait for His plans to unfold. God has waited for you for far longer than you could ever wait for Him. He planned for you since the beginning of creation but had to wait for your time in it all to begin planning with you.

"If we look forward to something we don't yet have, we must wait patiently and confidently." Romans 8:25

The plan is being revealed little by little every day. Take a step back from this moment and look back from an external view. You'll be able to see the ways you're already walking out God's plans for you and how every moment so far has brought you right here, right now.

Every building is made from numerous bricks and other small individual materials. Materials like thread must come together to make the carpet that will be laid throughout the building. Metal is melted down and shaped to create beams that will support the building and help it stand even in the wildest storms. All sorts of things are coming together to create a solid structure meant to last.

One brick lying on the ground is not a building but is still valuable. Each individual piece of lumber, wiring, or tile is seemingly insignificant if left alone. It is when the careful combing and construction of these materials occur that something grand and beautiful can be formed. Each piece plays its part. And even this must be done in prime conditions. It's hard for the foundation to dry on a rainy day, and it would be deadly to build during a hurricane. The builder would fare best building during a week of clear and warm weather; otherwise, he would have to expect delays or damage that could've been avoided by waiting.

"I want you woven into a tapestry of love, in touch with everything there is to know of God. Then you will have minds

confident and at rest, focused on Christ, God's great mystery."
Colossians 2:2

Every small occurrence, every moment of waiting, joy, pain, all of it, is being sewn together to form a beautiful and amazing tapestry. Stop viewing the individual pieces as worthless. It takes time to intertwine these separate pieces. Looking back will help you see how many of these pieces have already come together. One day you'll be able to step from behind this crazy-looking thing and see the glorious art that has been created all along.

In case you were still considering it, don't be the spork. Trust God in His timing for you. The time will come when you will be brought out to be a part of His beautiful tapestry. Stay resilient in your waiting. Being used up and tossed out is never God's plan for His children. Enjoy the process of being prepped for your special time.

CHAPTER 12

SEEDS

We are all given our own seeds. It is up to each of us to care for them. Some will disregard their seeds and toss them aside, saying, "I don't want an apple tree; I'd prefer a cherry tree because those are better." There are others that will keep the seeds but never plant them because, while the thought of having the fruit is nice, they don't want to get their hands dirty, do the work, then wait for the tree to grow. Another group will have good intentions. They accept the seeds, find good soil, and plant them. For a time, they may even keep up with watering the planted seeds, but eventually they give up because the seeds aren't growing fast enough. Seeing the same dirt day after day with not so much as a bud is disheartening—all that work for nothing. The last group, which is the group we all intend to be in, is the group that sees it all through, from planting all the way through to harvesting.

I've been in that second-to-last group more times than I have time to share. It's frustrating not knowing if your efforts will produce anything. Looking at the seemingly unchanged patch of dirt will make you feel hopeless at times. But here comes the need for faith again. Just because we don't see the growth doesn't mean it's not happening. It's just under the surface.

"Let's not get tired of doing what is good. At just the right time, we will reap a harvest of blessing if we don't give up." *Galatians 6:9*

Planting seeds is like a suspenseful adventure. You have to find the perfect soil during prime weather conditions. Before you plant, you have to put on the right attire—something durable that you don't mind getting dirty, along with gloves and a hat to give you shade while you work. You then till the soil, place the seeds, and cover them with the soil you just dug out. You water the soil and step back, feeling a sense of accomplishment and pride in what you've done. Now, if you want to reap what you have just sown, you'll have to be in the last group of people who received seeds. They plant the seeds, care for the soil, and faithfully wait, knowing that seeds grow down into roots before they ever grow up to bear fruit. They stick with what they have planted no matter how long it takes, and one day, they get to bite into the fruits of their labor.

"Meanwhile, friends, wait patiently for the Master's Arrival. You see farmers do this all the time, waiting for their valuable crops to mature, patiently letting the rain do its slow but sure work. Be patient like that. Stay steady and strong. The Master could arrive at any time." James 5:7-8

I recently watched a video that explained the growth of bamboo trees. This is the result of me scrolling through my phone when I should've been getting ready for work. But the video showed that it takes about 5 years for a bamboo tree to break through the soil and sprout. I don't mean 5 years to grow—to sprout. As in, it takes 5 years for that seed to grow its roots before it can ever reach the sunlight.

Above ground, it looks like 5 years of nothing. 5 years of the same. 5 years of returning to where the seed was planted and feeling disappointed at what appears to be a lack of growth. 5 years of fighting not to give up. 5 years of watering what looks like dead ground. 5 years of listening to people tell you that your persistence is crazy and not worth the hassle as they try to persuade you to start something else. It can be utterly exhausting. I think I may be a bamboo.

Every great and successful person you can think of has a backstory. No one goes from obscurity to greatness overnight. I don't mean the "15 minutes of fame" internet stars (even they have to put in a lot of work and post a million videos before they gain traction), but those who are doing something truly significant with their giftings. Over and over again, I have heard stories of the time between when God presented a vision with years between it actually coming to fruition. Mozart had a God-given ability to compose and play music, but that didn't mean he didn't spend years cultivating that natural talent that made him infamous.

God may have given you the vision to start a business. You're not going to hear that on Tuesday and just have it up and running the next day. Sounds nice, but that's not real life unless you're a billionaire with a whole business development team under your belt. But that vision is your seed. If you choose to plant it, you will first have to spend time with God to understand the direction meant for you. He will have to give you a glimpse of the potential of that seed.

You will find out what your business should be. Time will have to be spent coming up with a business plan. You may need to gather a team of trustworthy people to help you get started. Funds will need to be obtained, whether through fundraising or a loan. Even after all of this is done, you will have to wait for that business to get off the ground. Word will have to go out, so people will know what you have to offer. You could be an instant hit, but even as an instant hit, you may have put in years before that "instance." Or it may be years before you make it to where God planned for you to be. Either way, you have to spend time taking care of and growing the seed that was given to you.

A seed tossed in the trash is useless, but a seed put in fertile ground and properly cared for can become an entire orchard that will bear fruit that will be enjoyed for years to come. I know that some seeds end up being tossed because the one who received them viewed them as something to insignificant to bother with. Your seeds may not produce a business. They may not be for the American dream or anything one would consider to be grand. You may have a seed to go serve in the nursery at your church. Your seed may to get a group to take weekly walks. God can grow major things from the tiniest of seeds. Your orchard may grow simply from a desire to start moving in love and kindness. Then that little so-called insignificant seed could bring about the desire and ability to change many hearts. Don't count anything as too small to be grown and used by God.

I'm sure your wait feels long. What are you going to do? Quit? Sarah waited 100 years for the baby she was promised, and she got him. Anna waited about 100 years to meet the baby Jesus because of the prophecies she had heard, and she did (Luke 2:3–38). They waited and did not give up, although I'm sure at times they wanted to. They didn't roll over and die; at their ages, they certainly could have. There are points when you may want to give in and accept defeat. You may get tired of waiting and just settle for less. News flash! Quitting gains nothing but wasted time. If you're just going to quit, you might as well be like group one, which tossed out the seeds that were handed to them. What would be the point of hoping or trying in the first place?

Hang in there, stay diligent, persist in your faith, and hold on to what God has given you. Be like Sarah and Anna, who knew that the vision God gave was worth waiting for. Something lovely and fruitful will happen if you see it through.

Allow your roots to grow down and deep. Attach yourself to God's promises for you. Good roots spread far, deep, and wide. The bigger the promise, the more secure those roots need to be. Let some of those roots grab onto wisdom. Others will grab onto your faith. They should take hold of your confidence and the community you have around you. Be rooted in the planning and preparation. Spread out into all the good soil into which I pray your seeds have been planted.

Roots are an anchor system. Strong roots are why, even in hurricane winds, a tree will still be standing when that storm passes. If you'll relax in the waiting and let your roots grow deep, you will be able to stand strong in keeping your promise. You won't be easily taken down or uprooted. You will be able to dismiss the naysayers. You will face obstacles like challenges readily accepted. You will be able to see your way past right now into your future, and you will stand strong.

This marriage I have the pleasure of being a part of has amazing roots. I am fully aware that some of the things we have gone through are not for the faint-hearted. There are things about which I am confident that if we did not allow strong roots to grow, we would certainly not be together today. The roots and foundations laid by our relationships with God, the premarital counseling, accepting the correct wise counsel, and the habit of prayer have made us secure in what could've been disastrous. I'll take it a step further by saying the roots of things learned by allowing God to prep me during single life have come in for the save as well. Those lessons learned during those eight and a half excruciating years of waiting come in handy on a constant basis.

I thank God for taking His time to develop the unseen parts—things that we may never see or know that He has done behind the scenes that needed to happen for us to bear fruit. How can we bear fruit at all if we're not rooted in anything? Anytime the wind blows, we are knocked down, broken, or tossed away.

That same bamboo tree that took 5 years to sprout grows around 90 feet in just 5 weeks. I bet the marvel that occurred in 5 weeks made the 5 years seem like nothing. The wait is worth the result. The 5 years of growing roots gave the bamboo tree the strength it needed to grow rapidly and stand strong. If God can do something that magnificent with a bamboo tree, imagine how much more He can do with the children He loves. Allow your roots to grow down and branch out. When your time for exponential growth happens, those roots will help you stand strong and move forward into God's promises for you. You won't be easily swayed, and your faith will be strong.

CHAPTER 13

GET READY FOR BATTLE

Up until this point, I hope I've given you some great tools to help you walk through whatever it is you are trusting God for. But I don't know if you noticed that anytime God is about to have His people take possession of a promise, they go to battle. They had to fight giants, tear down walls, or go full-on to war. Whether you're speaking about biblical times or your life right now, the fight for what's meant to be yours is inevitable. The enemy will come at you with everything he has to try to hold you back or make you give up because he knows that if you push forward with God on your side, you will win.

Keep that in mind. You will win. You will win. And one more time for the ones sleeping in the back: YOU. WILL. WIN. God knows the plans He has for you, and He will not carry you into what seems like the wilderness just to leave you there. He will continue to carry you to the other side if you allow Him.

I don't know if you've ever gone house hunting, but it is a daunting task, especially in a crazy market. My husband and I had reached the end of our lease in the apartment complex we were living in, so it was time to go. The space was fine but did not feel like home, and we desired room to grow. It was no longer worth the price they were asking. Initially, we planned to buy a house. With what we paid monthly for our apartment, we knew we could more than afford a house. Just as our hunt was about to begin, my husband got sick, so I was looking at houses alone, which was not the way we planned to find OUR home. Then the lenders weren't giving us the number we wanted, and the market flipped to a seller's market. We could've called it quits, renewed our lease at the apartment, and endured another year living under a family of elephants.

We pushed forward and decided that it would be smart to wait to buy; that way, we could save for a bigger down payment to buy our forever home (we're too old for a starter home). I swear we saw every rental listing in our budget, and the end of our lease was quickly approaching. We put in an offer on one townhouse and got edged out by someone who applied right before us. We found another townhouse. He loved it. I didn't. But in learning to be a wife with the ability to submit, we put an offer in on the place and got it. Or so we thought. We began buying furniture for the place, and we were ready to go. That fell through because the owners did not renew their ability to lease their home with their HOA. Now we were in an "oh crap!" situation. Where we were living at the time already had a new tenant set to come in, and we didn't know where we were going. God did. By some fluke, I found this house that I was sure was still listed. You would often see listings that the agent forgot to take down. Our whole little family of four got in the car to go look at this house. It was beautiful and had far more than we expected for far less than what we expected to pay. That house is our home now. That is definitely a long story made short, but at each turn, we just knew that God had something for us, and all these obstacles we hit were just trying to slow us down and keep us from what God planned. He gave us a space where we could really propel our lives forward. Space for my husband's business; space for our children; space to host friends and family; and so much more. Now the price we pay is lower than the average mortgage in our area, which is wild. God always comes through with more than we ask for or imagine.

But we had to fight. That meant not giving up when it felt impossible. That meant not settling just because something easier was presented. It meant coming together as a family and praying for God to make a move for us. We had to maintain faith and keep God in the mix at every step.

That's just one example. We continue to battle for other things that God has for us. It's not easy. I know that, at times, running into these full-on war zones makes us want to just lie down and give up. Just go where the wind takes us. That is not a plan for the victorious. To be swept up like a leaf blowing in the wind is to accept defeat and remain defeated. That is not what God wants for any of his children.

Sometimes the biggest battle is going to be with yourself. We are our own worst enemies at times. The warzones in our brains are often the only thing holding us back from moving forward into the promised land, so to speak. We get scared. Get filled with doubt. Run through those destructive thinking patterns I mentioned before. But no more. It's time to advance. I think I'm a little fired up as I write this because I feel like I'm pushing through some barriers myself. Even in finishing this book, I let fear slow me down; I let the enemy whisper his lies about how no one would ever care to read anything I wrote. Why would anybody want a book from me? I'm nobody. I would get paralyzed in the process. I had to realize that I had been letting the enemy win. I'm not having it. Even if only one person ever reads this, I am doing what God asked of me. I had to wait for all the pieces to fall into place in order to put words down on the pages, but I do believe it was more than worth the wait. I hope you agree. The enemy is not going to steal me away from my purpose, and no matter what you're pushing towards, do not let the enemy take you off track. If you stumble a little or even suffer from extreme procrastination at times like I have, get back up and keep going.

Your battle may come from unexpected sources. When the devil is losing with you, that fool will try to throw everything at you, including the kitchen sink. Have you ever read the book of Job in the Bible? This is a prime example of the devil stopping at nothing to pull us away from God and His promises. Sickness, death, financial loss, and all sorts of madness. I pray to God that your battle doesn't look anything like Job's, but if it does, use him as an example. He never cursed God. He never stopped believing that God's ways were beyond him. And look at how God took care of him in the end, giving Job way more than he had lost.

Sometimes that battle comes because God is trying to take you out of your current place of comfort and move you into something else.

It doesn't matter what battle is ahead of you; you are armed to fight. I've laid out quite a few of those weapons in the chapters you've read, and they're all in the Word. You may need to be like the Israelites when they took down the walls of Jericho. You may have to go to your territory and march around that thing, crying out to God as you go around. You'll need to take up your two biggest weapons, knowing you will be defenseless without them: God's word (the Bible) and prayer. Be relentless in your worship. Gather some troops to go to battle with you. Bring in the best prayer warriors you know. Kick out the stragglers that only eat up all the supplies and slow you down. Be like Gideon and the 300 who were going to fight up against the entire Mideonite army (Judges 6 and 7). Only the ones willing to get down in the trenches with you and fight until you win should be running with you. Keep close the ones that will hold you up when you feel like you can't go on. I thank God for my family and friends who keep praying for me and with me. The ones that have encouraged me through every season to keep going. The army you fight with could make all the difference.

Above all else, remember the One who is going to lead you to victory every time. God. The way God comes onto the battlefield only requires you to be obedient and show up prepared. God will do the heavy lifting, and there are times when you show up and you may not have to lift another finger. The Israelites lifted their voices but never a sword against Jericho. Victory. Gideon and his troops simply made some noise, and because God was with them, an entire army fled in terror. That same God from back then is with you now, fighting your battles with ease.

The last and most important battle comes when God says it's time to go. You've waited. That's it. God just said now is the time. You have been prepared. You've done the work. You were obedient and trusted God to make things happen for you. It's harvest time.

When God says, "Go!" will you be ready to answer? Are you ready to drop whatever you have going on at that moment and run for the purpose He's placed in you? Remember when Jesus was rounding up His disciples? They had to drop everything and follow. Jobs, relationships, hobbies, and all sorts of stuff were left behind in order for them to start living out their purpose with Him. I do not want to be like the rich guy who thought everything he had at the moment was too big a price to give up what God had in store for him.

This should be the easiest part of the journey. For some, this is easy, but for others, this may be the hardest part of the fight. You may be doubtful after all this time. You may have encountered so many setbacks and false alarms that you aren't even sure if this is really it. You may even doubt whether or not God is really the one saying it's your time. Don't let me stop you from continuing to take just one more step in faith. Remember, what is yours is yours. You simply need to step up, take hold, and trust God to carry you in your purpose.

The wait may have been so long that you may have gotten into other things to fill your time. Are you willing to stop what you're doing and go?

I've used my singleness as a point of reference many times in this book, so it's only right if I share the end of that chapter in my life. I spent years being single, with a few blips here and there that are hardly worth mentioning. I kept myself pure, and like so many others who take that path, my wait felt like forever, and I often doubted whether or not I'd ever get married. Right at the end of my singleness, God cleared the way. Anyone who may have been interested in me was cleared out. I had gone through some major healing with God to repair the damage of the past. Once those things happened, I declared that I was going to focus on God and myself and not use any more brain space to figure out who might like me or who my next crush would be. I was going to be happy and take advantage of the gift of singleness.

I bet you might guess what happened next. Here came Calvin, stomping on all the little plans I had for myself. But I heard God. I heard God through the very short time we dated.

Then God said, "Go!" I was a bit scared. Even though Calvin and I met in 1999, at that point, it was 2019, and I wasn't sure if it was the right thing to get engaged after only four months of dating and married two months after that. My brain did try to fight me for like two seconds, but again, I heard God then and too many times throughout our courtship to deny that he was finally releasing me to become a wife.

I have to keep you in the loop about this writing thing as well. Remember when I told you that God told me to write a book back in 2013? That's when my seed was planted. It took another four years for me to hear God speak about the potential of that seed and receive the topic of this book. It is now 2023, ten years later, and I am just now receiving what I need to bring this to a conclusion. That time in between was filled with talking to God and getting into the Word to see how God felt about what I had been writing. But I definitely spent time in battle during this process. I spent way too much time psyching myself out by making myself believe that this would go nowhere. I procrastinated majorly. I got frustrated and put down writing for months at a time. But through all of it, I knew, and I know, deep in my spirit, that this is what God wanted me to do. Ten years after receiving the vision to write and six years after I began the writing process, I have come to the end. I feel that God has told me it's time to go. After all this time of waiting and working, I could just drop it here. I could say that simply writing it was enough, but that would be me moving in fear. I know God said to put this out there. Five people may read this, or five million may. It doesn't matter. God placed this in me, and He would not bring me this far just to leave it here. So, if you're reading this, you know what happened.

Don't get to the last step and give up. You ran the race; don't stop when the finish line is mere steps away. If God brought you there, He can get you through it every time. If you, too, are writing a book, finish it. If you have been working on a business, get those doors open. If you have been planning on going on a mission trip, buy that ticket. If you're thinking that it's not that easy, start again at chapter one and then do the work to make it happen. If you've made it to the end of your wait, don't let fear, doubt, or anything else take you out of the game.

God never fails. Never. He may not always do things the way you expect or when you would like them to be done, but He is always faithful. You may get to the very edge and feel like you're about to fall, but God is there with exactly what you need. You may feel like you are fighting an uphill battle for what you desire, but know that God is fighting for you. He's got His angels on the job, battling for your good. He makes all things work together for our good. Remember that.

Once you realize your waiting is an active journey rather than one spent twiddling your thumbs, you can come back to the scripture that is filled with so much promise and apply it to where you are today.

"For I know the plans I have for you," says the Lord. "They are plans for good and not for disaster, to give you a future and a hope. In those days when you pray, I will listen. If you look for me wholeheartedly, you will find me. I will be found by you," says

the Lord. "I will end your captivity and restore your fortunes. I will gather you out of the nations where I sent you and will bring you home again to your own land." Jeremiah 29:11-14

God can and will take you from where you are today and place you somewhere far better. He can release you from being held captive in the waiting room. "Hey there, the Father will see you now." Be ready to get up and walk in His promise for you, and don't forget to take it all in.

The End... Except it's really the beginning.